ACTIVATING
ASCENSION

www.activatingascension.com

ACTIVATING ASCENSION

A Guide for Living, Healing and Creating from the Heart

Dr. Kate Flynn, D.C.

Note: The philosophy, ideas and techniques presented in this book are not intended to be a substitute for medical care. Rather, they are intended to educate, empower and encourage its reader to be an active participant in the establishment of optimal levels of health and wellbeing. It is to be used in conjunction with conventional forms of care.

ISBN-13: 978-0615955612

ISBN-10:0615955614

This book was printed in the United States of America

To order additional copies of this book, contact:
Activating Ascension
www.activatingascension.com

Dedicated to the Power of Three

"*There are many forms and many faces, so that all may see, so that all may hear, so that all may feel the presence of God within.*"

~ AS

ACKNOWLEDGEMENTS

Thank you to Spirit for calling me into healing service and trusting me with this endeavor.

Thank you to my amazingly wonderful husband, who was walking this spiritual journey long before I came on board. Thank you for listening, even when I wasn't making any sense and for not having me committed every time I began a conversation with "this is going to sound crazy", or "you're never going to believe what happened today". Thank you for your undying support, your honest encouragement and for not giving up on me. Thank you for your patience, for pushing me beyond my comfort zone and for never trying to make me into something I wasn't or couldn't be. Together we are greater than the sum or our parts. I love you!

This work would not have been possible without the devoted and tireless support of Mary Jane Campbell and Denise Andrews. Thank you from the bottom of my heart for your willingness to help ground and anchor the frequencies out of which Activating Ascension has grown and evolved. Thank you for helping to make sense of the information and wisdom coming through and for always answering my relentless calls and texts, filled with requests for help. I am so blessed to have found you both and to be walking this journey with you. I love you!

Thank you to my older sister Christina and her husband, Wesley. Thank you for believing in me and for your kind generosity in helping to make this happen. Thank you for your unconditional love and ability to help me see the highest outcome. I do believe we have made Dad proud.

Thank you to the original sixteen who registered for the first Activating Ascension retreat, then known as Pure Energy Shift. I was shocked and amazed as each of you showed up and were willing to participate in something completely new and untested. You stuck by me through all the dramatic twists and turns this journey has taken and my heart overflows with gratitude.

Thank you to Mary Jane Campbell, Denise Andrews, Terry Flynn, Carol Murray, Carol Ann Redditt, Denine Savage, Karen Krogh, Emily Dameron and Maura Maloney. You have taught me the importance of sisterhood and supportive community.

Thank you to our children, Aiden, Connor and Julia, for being my greatest teachers, for pushing me beyond what I thought I was capable of and for helping to awaken the depths of compassion in my heart. Your presence in my life is a gift to be cherished.

Love and blessings to you all!

Praise for Activating Ascension Retreats

I feel that the timing of all of this retreat was very much meant to be. I had been "dog-paddling" in a stagnant place – trying to survive but not able to really live. This class really helped me push past blockages. I actually feel different. I have more of an understanding about the past negative situations I have lived through and feel like I am now able to move forward with more ease and grace. ~ EJ

Activating Ascension has opened my eyes to all the possibilities that lie within me and has also given me the keys to unlock and utilize that potential. I can already see and feel the changes within myself and, in turn, the changes I am helping to bring about in others. This is so powerful! Meeting all the people in our class was like having a reunion with long-lost relatives – a wonderful homecoming. I just can't wait to see all the wonderful changes that each of us are going to bring about and even greater things as a larger group. Thanks for letting me be a part of something so wonderful! ~ CS

WOW! This retreat was amazing! My life has changed in ways I had never before thought possible. It has helped me remove fear and numerous other roadblocks that had prevented me from being able to move forward in my life. I was able to quit my job of 26 years and start working towards creating the perfect life for me. With Activating Ascension, there is no limit to what we can accomplish! We will change the world! I have deep love and gratitude for Dr. Kate for sharing these gifts. ~ CB

I have been completely amazed by my transformation since becoming attuned to Activating Ascension. In mind, body and spirit, my life has changed dramatically for the better. Activating

Ascension has given me the tools to remove any obstacle from my path. I now believe that anything is possible! ~HF

Having experienced and taught many workshops over the years, I can say unequivocally, Activating Ascension is a life changer! While there are many techniques to clear long standing issues (some of which I have taught and used personally), the Activating Ascension techniques seem to clear on a level much deeper and more profound. Since the workshop, I have experienced a lightness of being physically, mentally and emotionally translating to life being more joyful and fun.

Not one to meditate regularly, I find myself wanting to and enjoying meditation…looking forward to the delighted experience. Lifelong issues with food no longer have the same impact. I am making better choices without conscious thought and have released weight without effort or struggle. I have also released the desire for alcohol and caffeine. Trusting the process has been so much easier. Amazing that for the release and clearing of issues, there is now a process that can and will change your life if you simply allow it. Activating Ascension, along with the love and support of those participating will catapult someone who desires change to new levels of awareness of self with ease! Thank you! ~ CM

Thank you, Thank you, Thank you!!!! My spirit feels so excited to hear and feel the answers to the deep yearning in my soul. I know in the deepest part of my being that this shift is real. Thank you for introducing Activating Ascension and Archangel Sandalphon into my life. I am so ready to help serve for the highest good of our evolution. How thankful I feel this evening. This energy shift is indescribable and so necessary for me to continue my journey. I have been so hungry for this. Dr. Kate you truly are a gift to us. Thank you!!!!! ~ DM

Contents

About Prayer, Intention, and Activating Ascension

Personal prayers and intentions are connections between your heart and Source, through which your reality is created. They are powerful requests for, and declarations of, transition towards your desires. They are said and lovingly released in the hopes that they will be answered and a favorable outcome bestowed. While prayers and intentions are ignited in the heart, they are often influenced by the ego. Without conscious awareness, they become laced with attachment and expectation. The attachment that the outcome will look a certain way and the expectation that what is desired will be granted without effort.

Understand that when prayers are said and intentions set, everything standing in the way of them rises to the surface for release. Allowing this release results in successful manifestation. Resisting this release will either delay the desired outcome, or completely inhibit it. Source will always respond to your request by giving you the opportunity to come into the alignment, or vibrational shift, required by it.

Consider the example of happiness. If your ego is willing to surrender circumstances and events it believes contributed to any state of unhappiness, then you will soon find yourself being noticeably happier in any given moment. If unable to surrender, everything acting as an obstacle to happiness will rise to the surface so that it may be healed and released. Situations in which you are withholding forgiveness, allowing resentment or acting from fear, will rise as each has a direct effect on your ability to be happy.

An egoic perspective will interpret this as a failed intention or unanswered prayer because it will seem as though what is being presented to you is too hard and requires too much work. Your ego may be tempted to go as far as to tell you that you are simply not *meant* to be happy. This is not true. Happiness comes through surrender. A heart-centered perspective will allow you to see each obstacle as an opportunity for healing and a stepping-stone to happiness. This process affects all prayers and intentions in a similar way.

Further understand that when the prayer or intention is dependent upon the free will choice of others (e.g., getting hired for a new job, selling a home or finding a mate), the course that will carry you forth will be influenced by their decisions. When one door closes, look for the next opportunity to open. By coming into alignment with your desires, a way forward will always be made available.

The gift of *Activating Ascension* is in the ability to identify each obstacle to your prayer or intention and understand what is required for its release. In this way, you know what to expect and are prepared to allow and create with grace and ease, from your heart.

INTRODUCTION

About Me

Hi, my name is Kate and this is one of the few times you will hear my voice speaking to you from the pages of this book. Up until six years ago, I never would have imagined that my life would be going in this direction. I grew up in a small town in Ohio that I couldn't wait to leave. I was born the youngest of four girls, to a mom with superhuman strength and courage. My Father died when I was two. As I am typing these words I feel his arms around me, offering a warm embrace and an encouraging word. Mom remarried when I was eight. It has only been since I've become an adult, and a step-parent myself, that I have realized the difficulty involved in helping to raise children who you did not bring into the world and who did not ask for you to be in their lives. Now, I believe my dad deserves a medal. Not only for staying, but for doing everything he could to show us the love of a father, even if we may not have been able to recognize it at the time.

High school was a time of constant struggle and conscious creation of chaos and mayhem because I could not find a more beneficial way to express myself, my feelings or the anger hidden

3

in my heart. So, I charted a path of self-destruction early in life. I like to think that I joined the Navy to follow in my father's footsteps, but that is probably not as true as I once believed. I joined the military because I thought it was the quickest solution to all of my problems. No one told me that I would be taking them all with me. Chaos and mayhem followed wherever I went for the longest time. I took solace in knowing that regardless of how badly I screwed up, I would never be in one place for very long and could recreate a new identity with a fresh background at the next stop on my adventure. I was unaware that there was another way.

My last duty station was on an aircraft carrier and I worked in communications. I was coming up for orders for my next station when I saw my name on the list of people who were being "automatically extended" for the next six month deployment. This initiated a wave of anxiety, because I could not imagine continuing under the circumstances I had created for six more months. I had initially planned on re-enlisting for another four year term, but decided to end my service six months early. I submitted a request for an "early out" and, to my amazement, it was approved. My terminal leave began the morning the ship left for its next deployment. My things were packed and I was ready for a cross-country trip, back home.

Feelings of uneasiness, doubt and shame started to sink in before I even hit the Ohio border. I resumed my job of waitressing at a local pizza joint where I waited on former high school classmates. This was a major lesson in humility. The universe always seems to serve up exactly what I need. Eventually, I went to work at an ink plant where my next-to-oldest sister was my boss. We pushed and triggered each other and eventually became closer than ever. Less than a year later I began working at a paint warehouse, moved out of my parents' house and left my home town. I breathed a brief sigh of relief, but it didn't take me long to return to old habits and chaos and mayhem reared their ugly heads.

Eventually, I settled into a stable relationship and completed two years at the local branch of Ohio State. I decided on a major of exercise science because I had always been interested in physical health and wellness. I had to move to Columbus to complete this program and was once again excited about the prospect of re-creating myself. I moved and the relationship fell apart, though he would be the one to encourage me to take another direction a few years down the road. Chaos and mayhem began to back off as I focused on my studies.

I viewed college as something to get through as quickly as possible so that I could start my "real" life. Happiness was an ambiguous concept, the actual having of it, kept just beyond my grasp. No one had ever told me that it was an inside job, so my outward search for instant gratification continued. I had defined happiness as a construct that would surely manifest after achievement. All I had to do was graduate from high school, serve in the military, complete my undergraduate degree and become a chiropractor. Then, I would have a career and happiness would be my reward, or so I thought. Turns out, happiness is something that happens in the moment when it's allowed. It's not something that can be sought after or a prize for finishing. In my experience, the more I've tried to force it, the further I have pushed it away. At Ohio State, I took as many courses at a time as I could and enrolled in summer classes the whole way through so that I could finish as quickly as possible.

I initially wanted to continue on to traditional medical school. I wanted to be an obstetrician and thought maybe I could learn something about life by assisting in the miracle of birth. These dreams were fleeting though, as I became aware of the state of women's health, or lack of it. It seemed as though women didn't really know how to take care of themselves. Maybe no one had ever taught them how. Or, if they did know what to do, they were not doing it. I began to reassess my intentions and what it really was I wanted to do in the world. I think as humans we often gravitate towards helping others in the same way we need help. I felt as though I was broken and if I could just help someone else in some small way, then maybe I would feel whole again. I wasn't ready for emotional and spiritual healing, but was drawn to the physical and structural benefits of chiropractic care. I felt that this was where I could make the biggest impact on helping others improve their health.

I enrolled in National University of Health Sciences Chiropractic College and moved to the suburbs of Chicago. If I had not been in such a hurry to get through it, I think I would have enjoyed the experience more. The course of study was rigorous and time-consuming, but it was fascinating. I loved learning about the body and how it works and the miraculous ways in which it heals when cared for properly. We had a small class and we were pretty close. I developed friendships that I knew would last, even as those from high school were falling by the wayside. I suppose that is simply how it works. People grow and evolve and if friendships and relationships attempt to remain unchanged, they fall apart. It's no ones fault and there is no reason to look for someone to blame.

I turned 30, got a puppy I named Phoebe, and moved closer to the city for my internship and last year of school. The chaos and mayhem began to subside even further when I got Phoebe. For the first time in my life I was learning about unconditional love. Though I was raised Catholic, I did not have a personal relationship with God. If I did believe, my understanding of God was as someone who took daddies away from little girls. This was the real source of my anger, even if I was unable to articulate it at

6

the time. Phoebe helped me see the light and the good in the world, even if I couldn't yet see it in myself. She also gave me a reason to be at home and someone else's needs to consider beyond my own. Even though everyone around me thought it was a terrible idea, getting her was the best decision I could have made. In Phoebe, I found redemption, the opportunity for forgiveness and the ability to love.

During this time, I received a surprise email from the boyfriend I mentioned earlier. Because of how our relationship ended, I did not anticipate ever hearing from him again. I learned that he had spent a year or two in Los Angeles and had returned back home because it was a better environment in which to raise his son. We decided to meet for dinner the next time I was in town to catch up. He is a kind, loving and wonderful man. His only fault was in loving me more than I thought I deserved. Relationships of that nature are doomed to fail. It was great to see him one last time and, before we finished, he left me with a gift - *A New Earth: Awakening to your Life's Purpose,* by Eckart Tolle. I don't know if he knew, but this book would forever and inexplicably change the course of my life, propelling me in directions I didn't even know existed. This book and a puppy formed a powerful combination, giving me the gentle push and unconditional love I needed to begin moving beyond what I thought I knew to be true.

Chaos and mayhem disappeared from my life. I found the God I was desperately seeking. He was alive inside my heart and always had been. It was only now that I could see, hear and feel His presence. For the first 30 years of my life, I was on a mission to clear as much karma as possible so that I would be adequately prepared for what was about to happen, fully emptied, and up for the challenge. Upon graduation, I took a job in Tennessee, packed my car, and headed south.

Introduction

I joined a practice that was not what I was led to believe, and I'll leave it at that. I almost ran home to Momma several times within the first two months and learned the hard way that one cannot purchase wine in Tennessee on a Sunday. After leaving the grocery store and the woman who loudly informed me of the law, I called my friend, Dawn. She had previously lived in Tennessee and was familiar with my predicament. She lovingly said, "Aw honey, you have to plan your drinking in the South," and did her best to console me.

I learned how not to rely on wine to see me through the hard times, while integrating what I had learned in reading *A New Earth*. I committed to a practice of purposeful prayer. I began asking God to send me a good man who worked with his hands, when I was ready and had fully released the desire to sabotage that which I needed most. My prayers were answered with miraculous speed as I met the man I would soon marry, a master craftsman, shortly thereafter. I decided to stay in Tennessee and was able to buy the practice, thanks to the extraordinary generosity of my sister and her husband.

During this time, my path was filled with the amazing women who would introduce me to energy healing and the intuitive arts. I was eager to learn all I could, as I had felt that the work I was sharing through chiropractic and nutritional care was, somehow, incomplete. There were missing pieces to the puzzle and I was on a new mission of self discovery to find them. I began with traditional Reiki and progressed from practitioner to master. Sound therapy through the use of tuning forks was next, and is still one of my favorite modalities to both give and receive. I learned Shamballa Multidimensional Healing, Reconnection, Emotional Freedom Technique, the Healing Codes and more. Every time I learned something new, I incorporated bits and pieces into my healing practice. I discovered Doreen Virtue and her healing cards, along with the work of Louise Hay, Donna Eden and Carolyn Myss and was inspired by each of them. The healing work I now offer to my patients has undergone several evolutions. Everything I have learned, in combination with what I have received through Divine guidance, has been integrated to provide a comprehensive approach to care.

Somewhere along the line, I began to hear very clear guidance and had a deep awareness and understanding of the Source of all creation and the many forms it assumes to become accessible. I became aware of the God innately present in all and found that wherever I looked for it I could find it. I heard God's voice in the whisper of the trees, the beauty of the mountainside and in the rush of the river. I connected with God whenever I looked into the heart of another and whenever I looked within. It was magnificent and omnipotent, beyond what I ever could have learned in a book or through conversation. It was the truth I had been searching for all of my life and I knew that I was a finite spark of the infinite. I knew that I am you and you are me, and that the boundaries of our physical selves provide an illusion of separation when, really, there is only oneness.

This is not to say that I have it all figured out. I still have my daily struggles and continue to learn the art of allowing and accepting and the beauty of compassion. Happiness is no longer an ambiguous concept and I am able to experience it in the moment, even if the moment is fleeting. I hold space that a beautiful and wondrous reality may be created, first within the individual and then cultivated by mass consciousness. I believe that isolation, separation, lack, duality and fear are part of a grand illusion and that truth is to be found in love, unity, abundance, community and power, through transcension of that illusion. It is my life's purpose and mission to share what I have learned with the world so that everyone may claim these truths, if they so desire.

Introduction

Through the acceptance of this mission, Activating Ascension was born. It was gifted to me from Source, in response to a prayerful request for a system of living that could be taught and shared with others for the creation of a new world. I am grateful for the opportunity and strive to deliver the message in its purest form.

 ## My Testimony

By this point, you are already familiar with much of my story. I would like to share a little more in regards to my experience with Activating Ascension. The birth of this system, within the time frame desired by my ego, required a steep learning curve. I learned through trial and error. Each error leading me to the next expansion of heart that would allow me to receive further instruction. There were periods of time where I cleared too much and too fast and went onto the next intention without regard for processing time. This resulted in weeks of feeling as though I would crawl out of my skin, unable to accomplish much of anything. I would celebrate getting out of bed and brushing my teeth.

Through it all, I learned. My destination-driven focus finally surrendered to embracing the journey and the understanding that the passage of time is largely irrelevant. Not to say that I didn't also learn how to mitigate undesirable effects or do everything possible to add efficiency. I learned the importance of a process for coming into heart-centered space prior to a session from the conflicting messages and resistance experienced whenever I attempted to release an obstacle without it. I learned the value in the completion of the closing sequence through the desire to release lessons learned, to be of service and to do what could be done to allow others access to the healing I claimed. I learned not to get stuck in clearing mode. If you're always looking for a red light, you'll miss the green ones that pop up along the way. Clear an obstacle and then move forward until confronted with the next one. Be in the flow. The most valuable lessons I have learned involve the ability to surrender, to know when to say when.

Activating Ascension has afforded me the gift of feeling comfortable in my skin. It has taught me to share the gifts I have been given without fear of judgment or rejection from others. It has taught me that everyone is doing the best they can to make sense of the reality with which they have created. The evolution of this system has led to a conscious awareness of a personal relationship with a divine creator, through which I am learning unconditional love of self. The result is the understanding of my life purpose and the confidence to carry it forth. And, it doesn't stop here, I am filled with excitement about what is to come!

Testimonials and success stories from those who have experienced Activating Ascension are interwoven throughout. Names have been changed to protect patient confidentiality, except where otherwise noted.

About My Work

Holistic Integration is the name of the comprehensive and multi-faceted approach to care I use with my patients. It is a gentle and focused way to encourage the natural unfolding of one's divine path that may otherwise take years or even decades. I work with my patients to determine their objectives, intuiting the balance between what they want and their soul's desire. The priorities that will result in manifestation of the objectives, efficiently and effectively, are then determined and a care plan is formulated. As you will learn in the context of this book, when alignment with higher purpose is attained, all that no longer serves may be released in an instant. To learn more about Holistic Integration and the techniques I use along with Activating Ascension, please visit www.drkateflynn.com.

In 2011, I was inspired to draw. Over the course of three months, I created almost 200 images resulting in four sets of Oracle Activation Cards designed to inspire acceptance, understanding and the release of all resistance to a heart centered connection. The *Illusion into Truth* cards helps you claim freedom from ego and the various ways that it is shadowing your ability to accurately perceive the truth. The *Expanding Awareness* cards are designed to assist you in coming into alignment with your divine purpose. The images on the *Heart Awakening* cards encourage you to release all defenses and help you to understand that emanation of your inner light is the only protection you need against outside forces. The *Nourishment* set helps you understand the importance of self care for a well nourished life. Each image is fully described in the accompanying guidebook. To learn more about them, please visit www.oracleactivationcards.com.

My current endeavors include the development and application of techniques and modalities to restore DNA to the divine blueprint so that it may be reconfigured for the evolution of consciousness. Scientists once believed that neurological synapses within the brain were "hard-wired", meaning that they were unchangeable. It is now known that this is not true and that there is a high degree of plasticity present within the brain and nervous system. It will soon be understood that this is true of our DNA as well. As our understanding is broadened, we move beyond the limits of what was once thought possible. This work includes DNA Restoration, DNA Reconfiguration and Blueprint Restoration. The more of us who are willing to hold space and work together to embody these activations of frequency, the easier it will be to progress. Are you willing?

About What is to Come...

What are you about to read is a system for living so that you may be able to internalize and integrate these truths for yourself. These words and ideas do not come from me - only *through* me. I was not chosen because I had already integrated them in myself but because I was willing to listen and had an amazing support team to help me discern the message in its purest form and with the highest degree of clarity. This platform for living and creating from the heart comes directly from Source, revealed to me in all its many forms, independent from religion or reliance on faith. I believe that there are many paths up the mountain we are climbing, and I pray that these ideas and concepts may serve you on your path.

I recommend beginning with Part I to thoroughly develop your intuition. Then, read through Part II until the Activating Ascension process becomes familiar. Study the techniques and choose a few of them to integrate into a daily routine. When you are ready, complete your first Activating Ascension session. Fluency in this process does not mean you have to do it all by yourself. Sometimes an outside perspective is necessary. Consider consulting with an Activating Ascension practitioner for assistance. For a list of practitioners, visit www.activatingascension.com. Proceed to Part III when you are ready to deepen your understanding of what it means to live consciously.

You will be receiving energetic downloads throughout your interaction with this book. I wish you well on your journey and I hold space for a magnificent transformation, filled with love and light!

Understanding Ego

To better understand the forthcoming explanation of ascension and its activation, you may first find it helpful to have a clear understanding of the ego, its purpose, how it is expressed and how to soften its effects so that you may better hear your heart. Ego is the mediator between your conscious and unconscious mind. It integrates everything you perceive into a matrix, or energetic box, comparing it with everything that has ever happened to you and everything you believe to be true. This matrix forms your reality and reflects back to you a model of the world, how it works and the most beneficial ways in which to interact. It is not objective because it is influenced by past experiences, social constructs, religious indoctrination, faith and more. Truth is as the individual perceives it to be, which is why individuals can collectively experience the same event and each have a unique understanding and explanation of it. Flexibility of this matrix is advantageous, allowing it to shift as the soul evolves. This results in tolerance and acceptance of those with a different or opposing understanding of the world and how it works. Rigidity within this matrix results in separation, isolation and a decreased ability to thrive.

The ego's primary purpose is to keep you safe. It is the ego that warns you not to touch the hot stove and to look both ways before crossing the street. It plays a vital role in your survival and ability to interact with the world. The ego is not something that needs to be annihilated, squashed or destroyed; it only needs to be balanced. When the ego is balanced, it willingly surrenders control and works synergistically with the heart to successfully create. When out of balance, in either direction, the ego will interfere with divine connection and the ability to live one's purpose. Too little ego and one will wither away in self pity, attempting to become invisible and unable to see the joy, love and beauty abundantly available in the world. Too much ego and one will similarly become separated due to the repulsion instigated by arrogance, narcissism and the need to be right.

Secondary expressions of an unbalanced ego include avoidance of change, an understanding of self through similarity or difference to others and a judgmental attitude towards self and others. The ego believes that the known, regardless of how unsupportive it may be, is safer or less scary than the unknown. It resists any possibility of risk. This is why so many people stay in abusive relationships or commit to unfulfilling careers and never reach their true potential. The ego is cunning and wants you to believe that, regardless of the possible outcome, it's better to play it safe than take a chance in a circumstance where you may fail or make things worse. The ego will do all it can to make you believe that it's better to stay where you are, unless the power of love overcomes it.

When constantly comparing self to others, it is nearly impossible to have a true understanding of who you are. Much energy is consumed in trying to be like someone else, while avoiding being like those with characteristics considered undesirable. This leaves little room for inwardly seeking the essence of your soul self. It impedes growth and enlightenment, as these are practices that evolve from within and radiate outward. This expression often leads one to the false belief that they must live up to someone else's standards or to societal expectations. Boys don't cry, beauty is associated with size and money is a measure of personal worth are all memes that propagate the illusion and further sever the connection between heart and mind.

When the ego believes you have failed at living up to standards or expectations, it attempts to make you feel bad about yourself. It may tell you you're not good enough, you're unworthy or that you are a failure. These judgments are often projected onto others when the heart is unable to overcome the ego. This results in a sudden ability to see all of the shortcoming of others as though you were looking at them under a microscope. It is easier to do this than to look within, accept your faults and love yourself anyway. Understand that, more often than not, those that are the most critical of others are often ruthlessly judgmental of themselves. On the other hand, the abundance of ego may mask one's flaws to the extent that the individual cannot perceive that they exist and are only able to see them in others. When the ego is balanced, judgment is released and the heart is able to love and accept, openly and abundantly.

The voices in your head, manifestations of ego, may be so loud that you may find it difficult to hear or feel the love flowing from your heart through an internal connection with a Divine Creator. The first step is to breathe deeply. Consciously thank the ego for all that it does and then shift your attention from your head and place it in your heart. Sit in the silence of this space and become aware of the love that is constantly flowing into you from a loving Creator. Allow this love to expand outward until the ego becomes silent and willingly surrenders. Activating Ascension is filled with more techniques and meditations to quiet the interference and improve your ability to live within a heart-centered space.

What Is Activating Ascension and How and When Is It to Be Used?

The primary purpose of Activating Ascension is for the surrender of ego and the creation of a heart-centered reality. Many of today's great spiritual leaders and teachers share a similar message. Use Activating Ascension as a bridge to internalize and integrate ideas and concepts that you know in your heart to be true (things like self-love, acceptance, forgiveness and the release of resentment) yet are externalized and unpracticed due to interference from your ego.

Activating Ascension is a self-empowering form of care, offering a path of discovery and a systematic approach to releasing all that no longer serves, in the form of obstacle removal. It is safe and effective and offers a place to begin self-facilitation of your care. You may use it as it is described or as you are intuitively guided. You may choose to follow the protocol step-by-step, adapt the opening and closing into your daily practice, develop a personalized energy routine to assist in balance and grounding, or use a technique or two as you are called. There is great flexibility in Activating Ascension and no right or wrong way to use it. Incorporate it into a comprehensive approach to the manifestation of your intentions.

Harmonious flow through an Activating Ascension session does require the ability to intuitively receive guidance and intuition development is the focus of Part I of this book. This section will assist those who are entirely unfamiliar with their intuitive self and will help those who have intuitive experience to take it to the next level. Focus as much energy and attention as possible into fine-tuning your intuitive abilities before continuing. Part II outlines the process from opening to closing of a session and everything in between. Familiarize yourself with the protocol, tools tables, session guide and techniques before attempting your first session.

Above all, relax. Breathe deeply. There is no pressure to perform or produce. Energy follows intention. So, if you set the intention to release all that no longer serves, including resistance, you will.

Use Activating Ascension whenever you feel as though manifestation in accordance with your truest form of self-expression is blocked or stagnated. Use it when you are filled with anxiety for the future or depressed about the past. Use it when you are unable to forgive or release regret. Use it when you are in pain or when you are ready to stop recreating the same unsupportive relationship. Use it to assist the restoration of health so there is no room for disease. Use it to improve the flow of abundance and to begin doing what you were born to do. Use it to create the life you were meant to live. You are so much more than you ever could have imagined. Tap the unlimited potential within and begin to remember.

To access the highest possibilities of reality, you are being asked to honestly see yourself, your relationships and the results of your thoughts, actions and beliefs. Are you willing to see that now, in this very moment, everything you are experiencing is a direct result of every choice you have ever made? Some were made consciously and purposefully while others were made subconsciously through an inability, or unwillingness, to participate in life. And, some of them were made before assuming physical form and enrolling in Earth School, when you collaborated with your Spiritual Support Team to decide what lessons you would choose to learn for the highest evolution of your soul.

If this concept is totally new for you, consider that you are a finite spark of the infinite and have chosen to incarnate into this world to experience the spectrum of possibilities -- from those you perceive to be very good to those you perceive to be very bad. It is through these experiences that you learn and grow. From this perspective, a more comprehensive understanding of life and circumstances is reached. Everyone on the planet is walking a path unlike that of any other. The key to a successful journey lies in one's ability to remember from where they have come and to transcend the illusory veil of separation, isolation and disconnection. This potential originates within a personal connection between oneself and a loving Creator. In this relationship, love of self transitions from ambiguity into reality. Love of self is then radiated outwards until encompassing all. In this moment, judgment is released, the ego is surrendered and the heart comes alive.

You did not get to where you are overnight. It has taken years, perhaps lifetimes, for you to accumulate the obstacles that are now firmly rooted in place. Do not attempt to release them all at once. Everything is energy and all energy vibrates at a specific frequency. This includes the experiences and obstacles you will be clearing. As your vibration rises, frequencies at the bottom of your vibrational range are deactivated, while higher frequencies are activated. In other words, you move up the vibrational scale in a range of thousands of frequencies. Small shifts in frequency are easily integrated with grace. Dramatic shifts in frequency are more difficult to integrate and may introduce turbulence, confusion and difficulty in your ability to interact with the world. For this reason, it is recommended to follow the protocol described in Part II as closely as possible. Once you've finished a session, commit to completion of your follow up and allow the clearing to be fully integrated before continuing. As emotions arise, allow yourself to fully feel them, so that they may be released rather than suppressed.

Activating Ascension is a tool to be used until instantaneous release, through intention alone, is possible. As obstacles are cleared, the path to higher consciousness unfolds. With every forward motion, the understanding that love is all that exists, evolves. Your ego successfully completes its mission, you get out of your way and your heart expands beyond what was once thought possible. In this space, there is peace. Pain and suffering become only memories.

What Activating Ascension Is Not

Activating Ascension is not a replacement for conventional medical care. There is value and benefit in prescription medications, surgeries and other medical procedures. I do not recommend you ignore medical avenues that could enhance obstacle resolution and add efficiency to the meeting of your health and wellness goals.

This book, and the ideas and concepts explored within, are not meant to serve as an introduction to energy healing and metaphysics. If there is a lack of resonance or understanding of the material, consult the suggested reading list found in Appendix D and considering beginning with Louise Hay's or Donna Eden's work. Once you have a basic understanding of energy, vibration and frequency, you will have a better understanding of Activating Ascension and will meet with more success as you work through it.

Activating Ascension is not the only modality to employ as you continue on your path of spiritual and conscious evolution to manifest your intentions. It is not meant to be a stand-alone approach and you are not meant to have to do it all by yourself. There may be times when you are too close to a situation and unable to clearly see things as they are. These are not times to facilitate your care. These are times to ask for and actively seek help from others aligned with your beliefs and ideals.

Activating Ascension is not a rigid construct to be methodically followed. You do not have to strictly adhere to the process to receive benefit from it. There is plenty of room for integration with practices you may already be familiar with as well as those you may learn in the future. Follow your intuition and do what works best for you.

It may be tempting to fall into the pattern of feeling as though there is more to clear before moving forward. Activating Ascension is not a place to get stuck. Clear obstacles as they arise, with the understanding that there will come a time when the only thing standing between you and where you want to be is a decision and commitment to make a new choice. Move forward in faith, knowing that you are fully supported in every way.

Part I: Intuition

Chapter 1: Intuition Development

Message from Spirit

Children, especially under the age of six, have a heightened awareness of an intuitive connection. Because the veil between worlds has not fully materialized, they are often able to communicate with angels, guides and other forms of spiritual support. They are able to remember a reality beyond what is consciously apparent to most adults. Many of these children are told they have an overactive imagination and are led to be believe that what they are seeing is not "real". As they continue to grow, the presence of their imaginary friends is discouraged or misunderstood and they are coaxed to give them up. They begin to accept the understanding that if you can't see it, touch it or feel it, then it must not be real. They begin to forget that they exist outside of space and time, finite sparks of the infinite.

This is not true for all children, and a few are able to retain these memories and communicative abilities. For the majority, the veil solidifies and as they mature their life becomes a constant quest to remember their inherent connection with all of life (beyond the superficial boundaries of physical form), how it feels to be "part of" rather than "separate from" and that the infinite source of creation flows through them and is limitless in power and ability. They begin to look for meaning in the outside world and, for many, their lives become desperate searches for truth.

The overwhelming frustration of this task may take a toll on the individual. Some will look for anything to numb the pain and fill the void of what they cannot remember. Others will turn to world religions and spiritual paths to fill in the missing pieces. The fortunate ones are guided to look within and find personal communion with a divine creator. The less fortunate are taught that God is vengeful and is to be feared. They live their lives feeling as though they will never be able to please Him and their actions are driven by guilt, fear and shame at the unworthiness of their existence. This is a description of extremes, the path of most, lying somewhere in between.

When a willingness to surrender and transcend the illusion of physical reality and a readiness to understand the truth coincide, the energetic balance is tipped and they begin to remember that everything they have been searching for was within them all along. Perhaps, you have come to this point. Perhaps, this conscious understanding is redefining who you are, being interwoven into your every thought, action and response. If this is the case, then this book has been written for you. The entire spiritual realm commends you for your willingness and our heart overflows with love and gratitude. The initiation of your ascension charts a path for others to follow, one heart at a time. This is how your world will be healed, created anew in love. This is how peace will be known and abundance manifested. We are here to offer assistance and support and to help spark the eternal flame of unconditional love within.

Introduction to Intuition

Intuition is defined as the direct perception of truth or fact, independent of any reasoning process. It flows from the soul-self or the aspect of self that is all-knowing. Everyone has the ability to receive wisdom in this way, though some may be able to tap into it more readily than others. Intuitive development is a practice. It asks for nothing more from you than to allow its expression. This connection between you and your soul-self is already in place. Wisdom, truth and guidance have been flowing into your subconscious, since you were in the womb. Intuitive development opens and activates these channels so that you are more perceptive of them.

Intuition is sometimes referred to as a "sixth sense" or a "gut feeling", allowing for the best possible choice to be made while navigating through life's circumstances. Take a look at your life and think about those times when you had conscious understanding above and beyond the available information. Were you able to follow your gut? How did your decision affect the situation?

In addition to a direct connection to Source through the soul-self, every human being is surrounded by an unseen support group of angels and guides, longing to impart wisdom and share possibilities. However, they may only do so through your free will request. Trust is required for this relationship to be cultivated. Know, that in their whispers, the voice of God (or a Higher Power, as you perceive Him or Her to be) may be heard. Guidance often appears in forms most accessible to the individual, meaning that if you are Christian, for example, you will be more available to receiving guidance from Jesus, the Holy Spirit or angels and saints than you may be from Buddha or a Hindu Goddess. Know and understand that each messenger represents the aspect of the One to which you will resonate the highest. They are all God.

Accessing intuition in the context of Activating Ascension is used to determine absolutes. For example, the obstacles to your intention are predefined. They have already occurred as part of your life experiences and are, therefore, identifiable. There are specific techniques that will assist you in the mitigation of these obstacles, offering a greater benefit than the completion of other techniques. In this way, determination of the most appropriate techniques to employ in your clearing is also a definable absolute. When looking forward, as in discerning the appropriate follow up or in determination of the action plan, there are definable steps to add ease and grace and bring you closer to your intention. These too, are absolutes.

The purpose of this distinction is to clarify the reason for inclusion of intuition development within this book. It is not included to assist one in the manifestation of psychic abilities for the foretelling of the future. Possible outcomes of the present moment are subject to an enormous number of probabilities extrapolated from statistical algorithms, based on the likelihood of personal will resonating at the level of divine will. It gets even more complicated when considering the effects of interactions within a larger community or group consciousness. All of this contributes obscurity to the vision. Release the need to have awareness of an outcome and, instead, focus that energy on consciously living in the present. It is within the moment that intuition is to be followed.

This chapter will cover the eight most common blocks to intuitive flow and how to mitigate them, discerning higher guidance from ego, tools and techniques for intuitive development, active versus passive reception and the art of asking questions. Use the information provided here in conjunction with the Intuition

Development Meditation found in Chapter 2. Develop a clear connection with your intuitive self prior to exploring Activating Ascension as it is presented in Part II.

Common Blocks to Intuitive Flow

Memes

Memes are opinions or beliefs that are assumed to be true, simply because they have been repeated so many times throughout a culture. Several examples that inhibit intuitive ability include:

- Accessing intuition is a direct challenge to God.
- If you have a sixth sense, you must be working for the devil.
- The only way to connect with God, or hear His voice, is through the approved religious text (e.g., the Bible, Koran, Vedas, etc).
- I can't access that part of me.
- People will think I'm crazy if I use my intuition.
- Or, people who claim to be intuitive are crazy.

Religious indoctrination has led many astray, convincing them that they need an intercessory conduit for connection to a Higher Power. This perpetuates the outward seeking of truth and magnifies the feeling of incompletion from within. Modern day society has been highly influenced by the unified ruling of church and state. For some, this is a residual effect of the past. For others, this is their current experience. The lines between spiritual truths and the need to control the masses are blurred, and then perpetuated over generations. Eventually, there is little understanding of the reasons for rules and rituals. They are adhered to simply because people think they should be.

Memes unaffiliated with religious implications have been largely influenced by cultural constructs, designed to belittle and make fun of those things that lie just outside of conscious understanding and unproven by science. People who claim to be psychic or intuitive are often treated as outcasts and are exaggerated and portrayed as freaks, liars and manipulators. Sadly, many live up to these stereotypes, helping to reinforce them. The truth is, as you begin talking with others about intuition, more often than not, you will be met with interest and responses such as: "Yes, I've felt like that before. I just never told anyone because I didn't want them to think I was crazy."

In understanding the nature of memes, the bigger picture becomes clear. They are repeated over and over again for the purpose of control. Anyone unwilling to fit the mold is labeled and treated as an outcast. However, times are changing and more and more people are awakening to truth. These memes, in particular, have outlived their purpose and are to be released through conscious awareness of them. To better understand the purpose or usefulness of a meme, ask if it is something that genuinely benefits the greater good? Or, is it something being used to deceive, control or disempower?

Discernment is the key. Bring each meme, belief or opinion into your heart. The above list is not comprehensive, consider others by which you may be affected. Ask yourself: "Is this true for me?" Focus your attention on how your body responds to the meme. When repeating the statement, does it open and expand your heart, or does it cause your heart to close and fear to rise? Statements that are true will cause your heart to open and expand. Statements that are false will elicit the opposite reaction.

Fluoride

Topical application of fluoride is generally believed to prevent dental caries. However, ingested fluoride may lead to calcification of the pineal gland, or third eye chakra, over long-term exposure. The third eye chakra enables the reception and interpretation of intuitive guidance. Calcification inhibits this ability. The type of fluoride naturally found in water is quite different from the fluoride added to water and toothpaste. One benefit of fluoridated toothpaste over fluoridated water is in its superficial application, rather than its ingestion or absorption. This helps decrease undesirable effects. However, both may be supplanted by limiting the amounts of sugar, dairy and processed foods in one's diet.

As you move forward, begin limiting exposure to fluoride. If your drinking water is fluoridated, look for alternative sources of purified water. Water bottled in plastic containers raises additional concerns, as chemicals from the plastic may leach into the water and contribute to other sources of bodily toxicity. Consider investing in a whole-house filtration system that specifically removes fluoride from your water source.

To mitigate the toxic effects of fluoride after it's been ingested, use the following number activation sequence (a complete description of this technique is found in Chapter 5) to unlock the decalcification codes within your pineal gland: **869127912 869 579128 5**. This is the universal code for initiating transmutation. Listen for additional numbers specifically attuned to your pineal gland and calcium deposits. Repeat daily for seven days.

Heavy Metal Toxicity

Heavy metal toxicity confuses your central nervous system and reduces the ability of your immune system to function optimally. Heavy metals stress the detoxification abilities of your kidneys, liver and skin. Often, they are isolated within fat cells or joint capsules because your body cannot figure out how to properly eliminate them. Aluminum and mercury are the two most common, though others may contribute to heavy metal toxicity and inhibit intuitive development as well. Common sources of aluminum include: cookware, antacids, antiperspirants, aluminum cans, paints and dental composites. Common sources of mercury include: dental fillings, mercury vapor lamps, polluted seafood and water, skin lightening creams, sewage sludge and vaccinations.

The protocol outlined below employs chlorella, spirulina, cilantro and bentonite clay for their natural abilities to chelate and bind heavy metals for elimination. Chlorella, spirulina and cilantro are natural chelators that bind with the heavy metals and see to their release through digestional elimination. Chlorella and spirulina are both algaes. Cilantro is an herbal remedy. Bentonite clay acts like a sponge, drawing out heavy metals and other toxins, either through the skin or within the digestive system.

Heavy metal detoxification may further challenge your immune system and should not be entered into lightly. Consult with a physician or natural health practitioner to plan and coordinate your detox. To fully release the strain of heavy metals, it may be necessary to remove dental amalgams containing them. Consult with a biodentist regarding this possibility.

Consider the following protocol for the release of heavy metals. Complete this nine week cycle, three times. Allow adequate amounts of time for rest and hydrate throughout.

Chlorella - 1,000 mgs, twice per day for two weeks.
Bentonite Clay Bath - 30 minutes soaks, for two weeks.
Spirulina - 1,000 mgs, twice per day for three weeks.
Liquid Cilantro – 5-10 drops, orally, twice a day, for two weeks.

Magnesium Deficiency
Magnesium is required for over 300 biochemical reactions in the body. Spinach, almonds, cashews, cocoa and pumpkin seeds are food sources high in magnesium. The daily recommendation for male adults is 410 mg and 360 mg for adult women. Very few have a diet sufficient in magnesium. In addition, magnesium levels are further depleted in the metabolism of dietary sugars. If you are guided to add additional magnesium into your diet, consider a simultaneous reduction of sugar consumption.
If you are finding it challenging to obtain adequate amounts of magnesium through your diet, consider adding it in supplement form. Magnesium orotate (an amino acid chelate), lactate or citrate are all highly bioavailable. Each of these will have slightly different effects. Experiment with the different forms and choose the one that is most compatible with your body.

Intuitive Flow Disturbance
You have an intuition grid (See Chapter 8 for more information regarding grids) within your energy body to assist the pineal gland in the reception and interpretation of intuitive information. When energy is flowing properly throughout this grid, intuitive guidance rises easily and effortlessly to conscious awareness. When this energetic flow is disturbed, intuition lacks clarity and is more easily subjected to bias from the ego.

Crystals may be used to encourage proper flow of energy within the grid. Complete the following meditation with fluorite, cyanite, obsidian, amber and moonstone. Place each upon your body according to the recommendation. Additional crystals may be incorporated to elicit personalized effects. Once the crystals are in place, lie quietly and allow the flow of energy to adjust. Approximate processing time is 10-15 minutes. If you do not have the physical crystal, energetically place it on your body with intention.

Crystal or Stone	Location	Purpose
Fluorite	Third Eye	Absorbs and neutralizes negative vibrations.
Cyanite	Front of Right Shoulder	Helps open psychic ability and enhances telepathic communication.
Obsidian	Solar Plexus	Removes doubt and negative thoughts, helpful in divination.
Amber	Sacral Chakra	Dissolves resistance.
Moonstone	Front of Left Shoulder	Enhances intuition and brings good fortune

Sugar
Dietary consumption of more than 50 grams per day of sugar will impede or distort one's ability to accurately receive and interpret intuitive guidance. To put this in perspective, there are almost 40 grams of sugar in a 12oz bottle of popular soda and roughly 30 grams in a regular sized candy bar. While the sugar found in these examples is highly processed, the sum total of all dietary sugars influences intuition. This includes the sugar found in fruits, honey

and maple syrup. Overconsumption of sugar also contributes to ill health, though that is beyond the focus of this book.

If sugar is a main component of your diet, begin reducing it. Make small reductions over time for lasting change and to mitigate any withdrawal symptoms you may experience. For example, if you currently drink four bottles of soda per day, reduce consumption to two bottles per day for two weeks. Then, reduce it to one bottle per day for two more weeks. Transition to one bottle per day and then one every other day, until you are able to completely eliminate it. Do not replace it with sugar from another source. Drink more water, green and herbal teas and healthy fermented beverages instead. Then, consider other sources of sugar and repeat. Start with the biggest source in your diet and eliminate them one by one, until you are consuming less than 50 grams per day.

Your intuition will improve, along with your health! If you are addicted to sugar, consider the cause. Is it an emotional addiction? Or, is there an imbalance in your immune system due to an underlying parasitic, fungal or yeast infection? Hormonal imbalance can also result in sugar cravings. Complete the Freedom from Addictions technique, from Chapter 6 and consider consulting a holistic health practitioner to determine the underlying cause of your addiction and to assist you in its release.

Lack of Trust
To be able to listen for and act upon intuitive guidance, it is necessary to be able to trust the source of the guidance and your ability to accurately interpret it. The opening sequence of an Activating Ascension session, Chapter 3, will assist you in coming into heart centered-space and help to cultivate this trust. Complete it whenever you would like to "tune-in" to higher guidance and it will improve your ability to hear and interpret clearly, thereby

improving your ability to trust that the guidance you have received is in alignment with your highest good.

When trust is lacking, fear, doubt and egoic attachment have an increased potential to pollute and skew the information coming forth. When clear guidance is received, it resonates in your heart as truth and you are able to move forward with ease. When bias is introduced, the information received will be muddled and you will find yourself re-asking the same question over, again and again. Awareness of repetitive questioning is a strong indication that you are likely influencing the information received. Return to heart-space, surrender ego and release attachment to outcome. Reference the techniques in Chapters 5 and 6 for assistance. In the meantime, repeat this number activation sequence to aid in trust development: **279819279 61799287 111 000 8 2971**.

Consider pulling the "Trust" card from the *Illusion into Truth* set of the Oracle Activation Cards (www.oracleactivationcards.com). Look at it often and allow frequencies that support your ability to trust to be activated, while those that stand in the way of the ability are deactivated. Remember to listen for additional numbers that are just for you. Complete the number activation sequence and interact with the card regularly to cultivate and nourish trust of intuitive guidance. This will also help improve your ability to trust life in general.

The following tools may also be used to prime your grid (Chapter 8) for foundational trust:

1. Visualize yourself in the center of a hexagon, sphere, intersecting trapezoids (however this looks to you), heart, and pyramid sequence. Repeat this pattern a minimum of three times, as often as possible.

2. Visualize white light flowing through your arteries and veins for two minutes, twice per day.

3. Visualize infinity symbols moving through your knees for 45 seconds, twice per day.

4. Before going to sleep, reframe daily experiences through your heart center, releasing all judgment, in a journal. In other words, record them from the perspective of your heart, rather than your ego.

5. Say the following number activation sequence to further activate your third eye chakra: **279182 79172 6957921 101**. Remember to include any additional numbers specifically for you. Repeat this sequence twelve times daily for two weeks.

Fear

Fear is the standard response of the ego when unable to logically understand and make sense of what is happening. Fear will permeate, color and slow your ascension out of ego and into heart, at every opportunity. Fear that you can't do it, fear that you'll be getting wrong answers, or fear that you're unworthy of higher guidance, the list of its possible expressions is long.

Understanding the mechanism of fear and how it is perpetuated will help you to release it more fully. Fear dislodges love, for the two cannot co-exist. To release fear and to hold love is a choice to be made within each moment. Releasing fear comes in knowing how fear gains access, how it is initiated and how it is perpetuated. The pattern is always the same. Fear gains access when vibration falls out of alignment with the heart. It is initiated by a false belief and perpetuated when consciously creating reality based upon that false belief.

The most beneficial way to diminish the opportunistic ability of fear is to recognize the potential for vibrational fall. Characteristics of energetic preparation for a fall in vibration include: increased heartbeat, shallow breathing, stiffness, confusion and irrational thought. With practice, you will be consciously aware of what is happening and will be able to stop the progression of fear simply by choosing love and coming back into heart space. To more readily recognize a potential fall, ask your higher self for a symbol that will instantaneously return your vibration towards love. Open yourself to receive it in heart-centered space and allow it to rise to conscious awareness. The symbol may be a representation of something tangible (e.g. a star, rainbow, sunburst, etc.) or it may be abstractly expressed in shape or color. Trust that whatever you receive is exactly what you need to be able to return to love. Meditate upon this symbol at the first signs of a vibratory fall. Consider completing an Activating Ascension session to further release fear.

Once love and truth are the foundation of your creation, fear can no longer be perpetuated. Ego can no longer trick you into falling out of alignment. Until this foundation becomes reality, there are tools to assist in the transmutation or mitigation of fear. Complete the following number activation sequence to activate frequencies of love and deactivate frequencies of fear: **8291657918 2 619719 2 82179 2**. Repeat the sequence five times, whenever feelings of fear arise. Listen for additional numbers specifically for you. Also, refer to the fear release technique offered in Chapter 5. Use this technique in conjunction with color, shape and sound to initiate a deeper release. There is also an image for fear release included within the *Illusion into Truth* set of Oracle Activation Cards to provide further assistance.

Discerning the Voice of Intuition and Higher Guidance from Ego

Discernment is the art of perceiving intangible truths over falsities. It is a sense of knowingness extending beyond what is readily apparent. In terms of intuition, discernment helps in distinguishing the source from which your guidance is flowing. Separating the ego's interference from the true and clear voice of heart-centered guidance is the first step in accurately interpreting what you are hearing, seeing, feeling and otherwise perceiving. Consider the characteristics of each, in the table below, and refer to them to assist in the development of discernment.

Higher Guidance	Ego
Always loving	Berates and belittles
Resonates as truth	Resonates as deception
Inspires peace	Breeds fear
Provides insightful wisdom	Magnifies reasons why you can't
Is felt in the heart	Is felt in the mind and/or solar plexus
Serves to unite	Serves to separate
Focuses on abundance	Focuses on competition and lack
Encourages alignment of divine and personal wills	Encourages personal will above divine will

Passive versus Active Intuition

Passive reception of intuitive guidance happens when you're not asking for it. It is the inspiration, or epiphany, that comes precisely when needed. It encourages and cautions, is responsible for chance encounters and brings with it a heightened sense of understanding of the meaning and purpose of life. Passive reception of guidance leads you down paths that would otherwise be left unexplored. And, because you are not actively expecting an outcome, there is no attachment to the destination. This allows the energy carrying you forward to flow effortlessly and without restriction. This form of guidance is invaluable in the benefit it has to offer as your life unfolds. However, navigation of Activating Ascension requires the ability to actively receive guidance.

The key to actively receiving guidance is found in the art of asking questions that have determinable answers (meaning, the answers are not subjected to probabilities affecting future events because they have either already happened or are happening in the moment). Questions that have clear "yes" and "no" answers offer a starting place. For example: For my intention of self forgiveness, would it be beneficial to complete an Activating Ascension Session? Questions of "how many" also have clear and definable answers. For example: How many agendas are blocking the manifestation of my intention? And, how many obstacles are contributing to each agenda? Finally, questions of "which ones?" will trigger your subconscious for the release of obstacles and will identify the appropriate techniques for your clearing. For example: Which obstacles make up each agenda? Which techniques will transmute this particular agenda?

Intuition Development

So that you may be able to easily hear, or otherwise perceive, intuitive answers to your questions, begin a daily practice for intuitive development. Remember, answers will be more readily available to you when you are able to be present in heart-centered space. Consider beginning your daily practice with the opening sequence detailed in Chapter 3. Integrate the Intuition Development Meditation (Chapter 2) into your practice, twice per month. An audio version of this meditation is available for purchase at www.drkateflynn.com.

Begin these practices while simultaneously releasing relevant blocks to its development, as described earlier. To determine which apply to you, write down each of the eight most common blocks, as previously discussed, on separate sheets of paper. Fold each of them up so that you are unable to see the words on them. After completing the opening sequence and stating your intention for their revelation, randomly select two and commit to their clearing and release.

Understand that all you seek lies within your sacred heart. In order to access and receive the wisdom emanating from here, your heart is to be trusted and open and a personal relationship with the Divine (God, Creator, Source) is to be cultivated. Consider the following sequences for inclusion into your daily intuitive development practice. Use these in conjunction with techniques described above to transmute blocks to intuition. Incorporate techniques from Chapters 5 and 6 as you are led. Commit to a daily practice and enjoy the opening of your intuition.

To trust your heart:

1. Repeat the following number activation sequence four times: **456892 71579 2 7 169712 57912 8 6**. Add all additional numbers specifically for you.

2. Complete the Intuition Development Meditation twice per month, allowing trust to build each time.

3. Nourish your physical body with fruits (2 serving per day) and vegetables (4 serving per day). This nourishment helps to free your spiritual connection from distractions.

4. Complete at least one activity, daily, that makes your soul sing. Dancing, being in nature, painting, writing, exercising, etc. Make a list of four or five activities that you truly enjoy and may easily be done.

To open your heart:

1. Repeat the following number activation sequence seven times: **8791265 79812 000 010101 7 297172 2791**.
Remember to add all additional numbers specifically for you.

2. Visualize your heart center filled with orange, silver and violet throughout the meditation and whenever connecting with higher guidance

3. Complete the fear release technique (Chapter 5) with the intention to release fear of having an open heart.

4. Complete one or both of the resistance release techniques

(Chapter 5) with the intention to release resistance to being open-hearted.

5. Repeat the following mantra seven times: **"In the now moment, I open my heart to receive. All that I need comes to me with grace and ease."**

To cultivate a personal relationship with the Divine:

1. Be in nature daily. Listen to the wind, the birds, flowing water, animals and whatever other sounds surround you.

2. Be in silence, daily. Do your best to clear your mind of distractions. Allow thoughts to come into your awareness and then release them. Begin with 5 minutes and progress from there.

3. Complete a prayerful fast, consuming only water for 24 hrs, once a week.

4. Declutter and simplify your environment. Attachment to material things stands in the way of a pure connection to Source. If you use something, keep it. If you do not use something, give it away.

Chapter 2: Intuition Development Meditation

This meditation may be completed all at once, or section-by-section. Read each part and then close your eyes and allow the visualization to complete. An audio version of this meditation is available at www.drkateflynn.com.

Establish a Connection between the Heart and Third Eye

Sit comfortably, feet on the floor and eyes closed. Center yourself and bring your attention to the space between and slightly above your eyebrows. This is the area of your sixth chakra, known as the third eye, the gateway to higher consciousness and the connection between self and higher guidance or intuition. Energetically place a sideways number three, like the top half of an infinity symbol, in this area. Allow the energy to follow your intention, knowing that it will.

Visualize or imagine 7 buttons in front of your being, vertically aligned and about a foot away. Notice how many of the buttons are buttoned and how many are not. If you cannot tell if they are buttoned or not, that is okay. Simply begin at the bottom button. As this visualization is repeated and your intuitive connection strengthened, some of them will already be buttoned and you will join the visualization at the first unbuttoned button. Focus on the bottom button and say aloud **"I choose to align my heart with my third eye so that I may be able to open myself to higher guidance and intuition."** Energetically button the button. Shift your attention to the 2nd button and say aloud **"I trust that the information that will flow forward is for my highest good and in alignment with Divine will."** Button the second button. At the third button say aloud **"I allow this information access to conscious awareness and I understand that it is flowing from an enlightened Source"**. Button the third button. Raise your attention to the fourth button and say aloud **"I accept this higher guidance as divine truth to assist me on my path."** Button the button. Move up to the fifth button and say aloud **"Feelings of peace fill and envelop me as my perspective is shifted and guidance flows through."** Button the button. At the sixth button say aloud **"I trust with all my heart the sacred bond between myself and Source"**. Button the button. At the top button say aloud **"I am one with Source and worthy of higher guidance."** Button the button.

Energetically place a white star, a red star, and a black star in a circle over the number three in your third eye. The red star is to help you stay grounded and in your body while receiving higher guidance. The white and black stars are to aid you in discernment and to mitigate ego. Spin the stars in their circle counter-clockwise and then clockwise. When the stars stop spinning the process is complete.

Shift focus to your heart center. Feel the rhythm of your beating heart and notice if it is strong or weak, regular or irregular, beating quickly or slowly. Use your breath to bring the energy of your heart into perfect balance. Breathe in slowly and fully, filling your lungs with fresh oxygen. Exhale even more slowly, fully emptying the lungs and ridding your being of stagnancy. Once your heartbeat is normalized, tune in to the version of yourself that has manifested optimum health and allow your hearts to synchronize. Fill your heart with love and gratitude for all that it does.

Energetically place a sideways number three, like the bottom half of an infinity symbol, in your heart center. Prepare your heart for connection with the third eye by infusing it with orange, silver and violet. However you see, feel or imagine these colors to be, is correct for you. There is no right or wrong way and energy always follows intention. Once the colors start to fade, or you have a sense that they are no longer there, the preparation process is complete.

The two halves of the infinity symbol are now ready to be joined to make the whole. Watch as each extends out to reach the other until the symbol is complete. Stay here until a strong connection between heart and third eye is felt. Solidify it with gold and silver diamonds all around. Heart and third eye are now connected. This connection will last longer and grow stronger each time this visualization is completed.

Band Removal

Bands are energetic devices you have placed around various areas of your body to keep from feeling vulnerable. While they do an excellent job of that, they also inhibit the reception of higher guidance. Each time this visualization is completed more and more bands will be released until there aren't any left and there is enough conscious awareness that no new ones are added.

Begin by removing any bands around your head. These bands cause undue pressure that may result in headaches, brain fog or sleepiness. If you can, get a sense of how many bands there are and how many can be released in this moment. If you don't have a sense of them, that is okay, simply set your intention to remove as many of them as possible. Energetically remove all bands to which you have access in one of the following ways: Visualize their disintegration into tiny pieces that are instantaneously transmuted into light and love. Ask that they be removed and taken away from you by whomever you would like to assist (Christ, guardian angels, or perhaps loved ones who have passed). Or infuse them with color, surround them in a shape and make a sound to release them.

Once all bands around the head have been released, move on to any bands that may be present around your neck. These bands serve to diminish your voice and may cause imbalances within your thyroid. Others may perceive these bands and think you easily manipulated or controlled. Release these bands through disintegration, assistance or color, shape and sound combination.

Bands surrounding the heart are next to release. These bands make it difficult for others to really know you. They keep your heart closed and make it difficult to experience true joy and happiness. They limit your ability to love and be loved. Choose to release them in any way you wish, now.

Focus attention to the area of your solar plexus, located between the bottom of the ribcage and the belly button, and any bands that may be surrounding it. Bands around this area may wreak havoc on digestion, causing anything from ulcers and acid reflux to constipation or diarrhea. They keep you in fear and tell you that you are not good enough. Release these bands now.

The sacral chakra lies just below the belly button and just above the pubic bones. Bands around this area stifle creativity and may demand conformation to a career, or other venture, that is out of alignment with your divine path. They also inhibit libido and sexual self expression, making true intimacy with another nearly impossible. Bands are placed here in attempts to hide deep hurts. No true healing can take place until they are released. They may cause issues and disturbances within the urinary and reproductive systems. Release them now.

The root chakra lies below the pubic bone and down into the area of the perineum. Your most basic and primitive needs reside here; the need for shelter, food, clothing and the desire to procreate. Bands located here set you adrift and disassociated from your body. They cause you to withdraw to within and perpetuate the belief that the world is not safe. They can make you accident prone and increase potential for disease, as their presence may interfere with your ability to be grounded and/or inhibit proper functioning of your immune system. Release them now.

Bands located around your ankles stop you from being able to move forward in a productive way. They may have you tripping over yourself, unable to make beneficial decisions and keep you stuck in places you no longer wish to be. You put them there because you were afraid to make the wrong choice. In reality, they make it so that no choice is seen. They may perpetuate instability within the ankle joints and make one prone to sprains and other injuries. Release them now.

Bands around your wrists serve to keep your hands tied so that you feel as though there is nothing you could do to change your situation or help yourself. These bands hold you at the mercy of others, as you look outwardly for direction and guidance. They are responsible for faulty programming within that says "I don't know what to do." They may result in wrist pain, carpal tunnel, weakness of grip and more. Release them now.

Become aware of how your body feels without the constriction of these bands. Notice how energy flows through steadily and evenly as stagnancy is released. Make the conscious decision to free yourself of all bands and to never place them again.

Higher Self Connection

There is an aspect of yourself that watches over your physical being. This may be known as soul self or higher self. A connection with this aspect provides a channel for intuition and higher guidance to flow. Begin by visualizing or imagining this aspect of you. What does he or she look like? How do you imagine him or her to be? Make a heart-to-heart connection with this aspect of yourself through three intertwined threads of white, yellow and silver light.

Strengthen this connection by infusing it with love. Know that this aspect of yourself is always watching over you, loving you and supporting you in any way possible. This aspect of you is the filter through which all higher guidance or intuition will flow. Thank your higher self for all he or she does and send energy to this connection often.

Connecting with Source

Once connected to your higher self, a connection to Source will come easily and effortlessly. The connection will be initiated with the following number activation sequence: **2691 715798 162579 79172**. As always, remember to listen for and allow access to all additional numbers coming into your field that are specific to you. Once the sequence is complete, say aloud **"I wish to be in constant communion with Source and access all that has ever been, all that is and all that will ever be."** Wait for the light connection to be made and place a sphere at the top and bottom of the connection, allowing them to rotate in opposite directions, keeping the flow of information always moving.

Decompartmentalization

Your experience has, at times, pushed you beyond what you perceived you could handle and caused you to put up barriers and compartmentalize aspects of yourself to keep them separate from the whole. In this way, you become disjointed and intuitive flow is inhibited, diluted or distorted.

Imagine that you are a house. What does your house look like? Is it open and spacious, filled with lots of sunlight? Or is it dark and closed off from the sun? Are there a few easily accessible rooms? Or are there several rooms with nooks and crannies in which to hide? Imagine that your house is undergoing massive renovations. All non-load bearing walls are coming down. Support walls stay in place, but no one room is completely separated by another. Look at your house. Stand in the middle of the house that is you in all of your glory. See your shadow side and your light side coming face to face and meeting for the first time. Introduce them to each other and welcome all of them into your heart with unconditional love. Accept your shadow side, knowing that it is part of being human to experience the spectrum of all that is. It is from our shadow side that our learning and spiritual evolution occur. This is what allows you to shine your light even brighter.

Release all of your secrets to the light. Bask in the glory of God, Creator or Source, knowing that you are worthy of love, guidance and support.

Unification and Integration

Unification and integration of all that was decompartmentalized will happen now. This will take a few moments. You may feel flushed or warm as circulation is improved. Energy flowing through acupuncture meridians that were previously gated will now flow uninhibited. This energy is ushering in a higher vibration and will burn through lower vibrations that are out of synch with your new state of being. You are being attuned to a higher state of consciousness. Intuition and higher guidance are well within reach.

Awakening Higher Senses

Steady yourself in your knowing that you are one with all-that-is. Take in a deep breath and bathe yourself in ancient wisdom. Accept responsibility for all you came to this planet to create. Choose to move forward in a heart-centered way and always listen for the inner voice to guide your path. Moving forward in darkness is no longer an option. Relying on outward guidance is to deny your truth, your power and your mastery. You came to transcend the illusion, to remember the connection and to help others to do the same. The time is now.

Removing Armor

Armor placed around the heart to keep others out, to keep self in, or to maintain isolation must now be removed. Thinking that your heart needs to be protected is part of the great illusion and slows the flow of intuitive guidance. Understand that it is now more important than ever to have an undefended heart that stays open regardless of life circumstances. One open heart holds the space for 500 others to release their armor and open their hearts. Imagine the possibilities!

Keep in mind that there may be up to seven layers of armor surrounding your heart. Remove them slowly, one per visualization, so that the shifts are easily integrated into your being. Loosen the bonds holding the outer layer in place with color. This will be different for everyone. Simply allow the color or colors to appear, knowing that you have set your intention and that it will be done. Once the outer layer has been loosened, call upon Divine assistance to help you take it off. Take a moment to reflect upon the armor and the experiences that led to its placement. Fill it with love and gratitude for all it taught you and then release it. Allow your assistants to take the armor away to be transmuted into pure light and love. Use a blue-violet flame to disintegrate any energetic cords or threads attaching you to the armor. An open heart provides an abundance of safety and security for those willing to release attachment and stop keeping score.

Planetary Connections

Planetary connections amplify and stabilize the intuition grid present within each of us. The connections that will take place are energetic in nature. There is nothing for you to do, simply set your intention and allow. Inhale deeply and initiate your planetary connection with Mercury. Align with its desire to improve communication and heighten clairaudient abilities to better hear higher guidance. This connection will appear as a mixture of silver, blue and green. There is a volume control dial that may be adjusted according to your command. Adjust it now.

Inhale deeply and initiate your planetary connection with Venus. Align with its desire to purify your heart and mind and to refine intuitive flow from higher guidance so that you may receive the highest information with as much clarity as possible. This connection will be felt or otherwise sensed in your third eye. From your third eye it will wash over your entire being. Accept purification and refinement into your heart.

Inhale deeply and initiate your planetary connection with Earth. Align with its desire to ground your energies deep into its core, to bring about balance between the physical and ethereal planes, and to nourish. This connection will surge upwards through the bottoms of your feet, up the center of your body and into your heart where it will merge with Source energy.

Inhale deeply and initiate your planetary connection with Mars. Align with its desire to give you courage to focus and realize the intuitive and psychic abilities that are innately yours. This connection will come directly into your heart and spread outward from there. Trusting of the heart is a decision that needs to be made. Decide to trust your heart and all of the wisdom that lies within.

Inhale deeply and initiate your planetary connection with Jupiter. Align with its desire to open, expand and inspire your intuitive connection with higher guidance. This connection will be found around your waist and will surround each cell of your being with limitless pathways of communication. Feel the love and support of Jupiter wishing you well on your journey. Jupiter will always help you find your way.

Inhale deeply and initiate your planetary connection with Saturn. Align with its desire to instill discipline and to help you set limits and mark boundaries. Saturn offers a caution not to live in the spiritual world in an imbalanced way that may be detrimental to the physical body. This connection is a reminder that you still have free will. Less than 50% of your path is predetermined. When it feels as though no wisdom is flowing from higher guidance, understand that you get to choose what you would like to create.

51

Inhale deeply and initiate your planetary connection with Uranus. Align with its desire to inspire inventiveness, freedom of expression and life changes in accordance with Divine path. Uranus offers the green light to manifest from heart-centered creation. What would you like to create? What does it look like? How does it feel? Use the green light from Uranus to make it reality.

Inhale deeply and initiate your planetary connection with Neptune. Align with its desire to reveal the God within and the God in others. Allow Neptune to amplify psychic and mystical powers and to raise your cosmic consciousness. This connection will begin in the crown chakra and rain down into the auric field. Light and dark purple exemplify this connection and may be seen or otherwise sensed.

Inhale deeply and initiate your planetary connection with Pluto. Align with its desire to help you face your deepest secrets and bring your shadow side to the light. Release the old that no longer serves and be born again in truth and love. Connect with Pluto whenever questions of discernment arise. The shapes of this connection are stars, hearts, and clovers. Allow them into your field now.

Cord Release

Cords are energetic ties that hold you in attachment to other people, places, things or times in unbeneficial ways. All that is holding you back and keeping you from accessing intuition and higher guidance must now be released. Visualize, feel or otherwise sense any and all cords coming from your being and attaching you to old beliefs and the control of your ego. Bring them together in a bundle in front of you. Pass a blue violet flame in between you and all that is ready to be released, allowing the cords to completely disintegrate and be transmuted into pure light and unconditional love. Each time you complete this meditation, more and more cords attaching you to ego will be released. Surrender to Source.

Creating Wholeness

Become consciously aware of anything in your field or physical being that does not belong to you and no longer serves your highest good. Set your intention to release these pieces, return them to their rightful owners and release them lovingly and with gratitude. Trust that they will be made healed and made whole and easily integrated where they belong.

Become consciously aware of anything that belongs in your field or physical being that is missing. Energetically call these pieces back to you, healed and made whole, and allow them to be integrated into your being with ease and grace in the now moment for your highest good.

Begin to offer up any pieces you may have that are wounded or bind you to fear. Release these pieces to the Divine, trusting that they will be healed and made whole, transmuted into light and love. The pieces that will help you on your forward path will be returned over time. The pieces that no longer serve will be forever in the Creator's care. Feel the freedom that comes with this. Releasing attachment to your story makes room for grace. Breathe.

Power Reclamation

It is time to reclaim your power. Use a white star spinning clockwise to create the necessary space within you on a cellular level. Once the space has been created, send a silver and blue beacon up and out through your crown chakra. Energy follows intention, so as long as you intend to do so, it will be done. The beacon will be activated with the following number sequence: **862975 114927**. Listen for additional numbers now. Send the beacon out in all directions, dimensions and realities. Allow your power to come into your cells gently and slowly, transmuted in love, with ease and grace in the now moment. Seal it in by setting your intention that you will always choose to shine your light.

Installation of Trust

Request that the frequency of trust be implanted and interwoven within the third eye and heart connection. Over time, and with repetition of this meditation, doubt, the need to second guess and misperceptions pertaining to intuition will significantly diminish. All that is necessary is to have an open heart. Implantation of these frequencies will occur in three phases. In the first phase, neuronal connections within the third eye will be made more efficient. The second phase will prime the electrical system of the heart. In the final phase the two will be bridged with frequencies of trust.

Merging Energy Streams

Visualize or imagine a stream of energy moving you forward on the intuitive path. Notice if it is a rushing river or a trickling stream. Follow the river back and look for any divergent tributaries coming out from it. Surround and infuse each divergent stream with love and ask it to merge with your intuitive river. Complete this process until there are no more divergent streams and the energy carrying you forward is a rushing river.

Soul Star Alignment

The soul star or eighth chakra is located above the crown chakra. It is separated from the crown by the stellar gateway. When the three of these are aligned, access to infinite wisdom is granted. Use intention to focus their openings so that they are directly over each other. Send a beam of light up and out through your crown chakra, thread it through the stellar gateway and up to the soul star. Once the beam of light is straight and you are able to visualize or sense that it has passed through the crown, stellar gateway and soul star, alignment has been reached.

Unlocking the Sixth Sense

Your intuition and connection with higher guidance has been waiting for you. There is only one thing left to do. Ask divine assistance to provide you with a key to unlock it. Trust that whatever is given to you is exactly what you need. Use the key and turn the lock. Accept your intuition lovingly into your being. Use it for the greater good and understand that with great power comes great responsibility.

Allison

Allison was referred to me by the wonderful owner of a local yoga studio. She has scoliosis and had been under the regular care of a chiropractor for several years. Since she was happy with the care he was providing I suggested that she stay with him for adjustments and we would focus our efforts on the energetic level. Allison's primary intention was to release depression. She was working in a stressful position, helping to care for others while barely able to care for herself.

We had several intensely emotional sessions. All but forgotten situations and experiences from the past came up to the surface to be released. During this time, her father fell ill. Through all of this, we made steady progress. For the first time in a long time, Allison was able to sleep and her bowels began a regular pattern of elimination.

On our fifth visit, I asked her how her back was feeling. Her response, as confusion spread across her face, "It hasn't bothered me since we began this work. It's really odd, I've been so used to needing to go in for an adjustment every three weeks, like clockwork. Now, I don't feel like I even need it." Physical pain is often an extension of our emotional state.

Part II: Activating Ascension

Chapter 3: Opening an Activating Ascension Session

The Opening Sequence

Healing work and intuitive interpretation of guidance will be of a higher vibration when you come into heart-centered awareness and are in connection with the Creator, in the purest form. The following sequence was designed for the Activating Ascension system, though it is a wonderful way to open any healing session or intuitive reading. These steps ensure that you are surrounded by energies that wish to assist you on your journey and create the space for purity of heart, while limiting the influences of ego. By completing the following steps before your sessions, attachments and biases will be kept to a minimum. The words for each step are simply recommendations. Use them as a point of reference and allow them to evolve so that they speak directly to you. Say the words each time, until they become the definition of the step. Once that connection is forged, no words will be necessary.

For example, Opening a Sacred Circle is the first step. In the beginning it will behoove you to state what it means to open circle, whether or not you use the words below or some version of them.

Over time and with repetition, you may choose to simply say: **"Let us open a sacred circle."** In the beginning, it will take you a few moments to complete the opening sequence and come fully into heart-centered space. With practice, this will happen automatically with your intention. The energy of the words will be programmed and integrated into your intention.

Opening a Sacred Circle

A whole team of light beings, angels, guides, ascended masters and more, surround you at every moment, waiting to assist in any way. They long to share their love, wisdom, knowledge and encouragement so that you are fully supported. Free will deems it necessary to ask for their assistance before they can give it. Opening a sacred circle is a wonderful way to invite them in and let them know that their guidance is desired and appreciated. Gratitude has an extremely high vibration and allows the transition into heart-centered space to be made easily.

Prior to opening your sacred circle, you may choose to close your eyes and breathe deeply. Release your mind from any thoughts, worries and concerns for the day. Become fully present in the moment and set the intention that your heart be open and ready to receive.

To open a sacred circle: "I am here today for communion with the divine that I may receive all that is offered to me with purity of heart, mind, body and soul. I invite all beings of light and energies of high vibration to impart love, wisdom and guidance so that I may manifest the ultimate expression of human form. I request this with deep gratitude and appreciation."

Establishing a Pure Connection

Discernment, the art of interpreting inner truth, is a valuable tool. Not only is it beneficial to know exactly where your guidance is coming from, it is also helpful to have the clarity to receive it in its purest form. After opening your sacred circle, surrender your ego and allow for the establishment of a pure connection between yourself and Source. This step releases you from third dimensional consciousness and allows Christ consciousness to emerge.

Say: "I allow for the establishment of a pure connection between myself and Source, freed from ego. I welcome all knowledge, wisdom and insight. I lovingly release anything that may be interfering with the accurate perception of guidance coming to me, for my greatest good. Please assist me in being a clear channel, that I may receive the support offered, in its highest form."

Sacred Heart Connection

Your sacred heart is the space within, where the human aspect of you intersects with your soul self, Source and with the heart of the Earth. Your heartbeat is both a tangible and metaphorical symbol of the life that flows within you. It is linked to the Earth's heartbeat and the life-force that flows within the planet. Both have been evolving, as consciousness chooses to release the veil and accept the truth. The Earth is paving the way for this evolution to occur and your heartbeat is inextricably linked to hers. Allow this energetic connection to guide you on the forward path. Awareness of this brings peace, harmony and flow. Where this connection intersects with Source, in your heart, the understanding of truth opens infinite potential.

It is here, in your sacred heart, that you will experience a growing awareness of this connection between you, the Earth and Source. This creates the space for heart-centered reception of wisdom, guidance and truth. This inhibits your ego from filling your awareness with fear and falsities. Your soul's purpose is revealed through this sacred heart connection.

Coming into Sacred Heart: Close your eyes and intentionally come into your sacred heart. Visualize the color green, the color of pure and unconditional love, inside this space. Come into alignment with its energy. Allow its light to expand outward from your heart, growing larger and larger with every breath. Stay here until a strong connection with your sacred heart is created. Know that all of the answers you seek are waiting for you here. With this connection in place, surround yourself with a merkaba (a three dimensional Star of David). Allow the upward facing pyramid to begin slowly rotating in the counterclockwise direction. Allow the downward facing pyramid to begin slowly rotating in the clockwise direction. Intend that these remain here with you, throughout your session.

Setting Intention

Your intention determines which obstacles and agendas (more to come about these) will be available for clearing in this session. There are infinite possibilities for your intention. They may be focused at the physical, mental, emotional or spiritual level of your being. If you feel as though your life is "stuck" in a generalized way, you may simply set your intention to clear that which needs to be cleared so that you may become unstuck, able to move forward in a new way and have more clarity surrounding what you would like to create.

If you find yourself saying things like "I don't care", "it's up to you", "whatever you decide is fine with me" or "it doesn't matter to me" on a regular basis throughout your daily life, you may find setting an intention to be a little troublesome. This process is all about you! No one can step in and make these decisions for you. In fact, if you want to be honest with yourself, consider a few circumstances in which your response was similar to the examples above. Was it really true that you did not care what decision was made? Or, was there something you would have liked to have said, an opinion you would have liked to share for consideration, but didn't? Now, consider why you were unable to speak your truth. Were you afraid to upset the status quo? Were you trying to make everyone else happy by keeping your desires quiet? Were you worried that someone else's ideas were going to be better than yours, so, rather than take a chance, you submitted to what they wanted to do? If any of these patterns ring true to you, make the commitment to voice your thoughts, ideas and desires, now. Committing to do so does not mean that you get to dictate all decisions being made. It simply means you are willing to voice your opinion. You are allowing yourself to be heard. In life experiences, you get to have a say! You are worthy! You are good enough! And, your thoughts and ideas deserve to be heard and respected. If this applies to you, practice "speaking up" on your behalf.

As mentioned above, there are infinite possibilities for your intention. Consider specific areas of your life where you feel as though you are blocked from moving forward or creating in a new way. This could be in the case of a physical symptom or disease process. Very often, there is a large energetic component contributing to these. For example, have you ever had physical pain that came on gradually, had no correlation to physical trauma and worsened over time? Things like this are your body's way of trying to tell you something. Consider what was going on in your life when the symptoms or disease process began. Were you mourning the loss of a loved one? Recently divorced? Found out you couldn't have children? Assumed the role of caretaker for a parent or relative? Moving beyond the physical allows the true source of things like pain, discomfort or disease to be revealed.

Even when there is a correlation with trauma, it is a good idea to look at any mental, emotional or spiritual components For instance, consider whiplash after a car accident. On the surface, it seems as though any pain following the accident would be 100% physical in nature. This could be verified through X-Rays and Cat Scans, loss of mobility and the need for pain medications. If this was true, how do you explain those rare situations in which people have walked away from such accidents with absolutely no pain whatsoever? Why do some continue to struggle with chronic pain and attribute every flare up or exacerbation to the accident they were in fifteen years ago, even though the body completely regenerates itself every seven years? Why does their cellular memory keep creating a cell that experiences the same pain over and over again, while others are able to walk away from that same type of accident and not develop chronic degeneration? To answer simply, those who fully recovered were able to process through the accident on all levels. They were able to accept the experience, forgive those involved and ultimately release it. Those with chronic implications were unable to do so. The good news is, it's never too late. These tools, and others like them, can assist you in a full release, regardless of how long ago the injury was incurred.

Examples of things that have been physically manifested and may be energetically released with Activating Ascension include: pain release, insomnia, constipation/diarrhea, headaches, acid reflux, sinus congestion, gout, diabetes, menopause, gallbladder attacks, liver disease, cancer, etc. Beyond the physical processes, each of these issues has an energetic component. Using the Activating Ascension system in conjunction with medical and alternative care will drastically improve your prognosis.

Moving beyond physical experiences you may like to release or see improved, in what other areas of your life would you like to see a positive change? Perhaps you would like to clear any obstacles standing in between you and your romantic partner? Either for attraction of a wonderful partner or for improving your relationship with an existing one. Would you like to see your financial situation improve and clear any obstacles resulting in poverty consciousness? Perhaps you would like to transition out of your nine-to-five job and start a business? With the removal of obstacles, the way forward will be seen and the manifestation of your intention becomes possible. In this moment, make a list of all areas of your life that you would like to be creating differently. Do not allow your ego to limit your possibilities. Now, feel into each item on your list. When you get to the one that elicits the biggest reaction in your heart, you have found the intention upon which to focus first.

To set your intention: "I have opened this sacred circle to ask for divine assistance in helping me _____. I set my intention to clear anything that is blocking my progress. Open my eyes to see that which needs to be seen so that I may move forward with clarity. Help me to do so with ease and grace in the now moment."

Opening Prayer

In lieu of setting an intention, you may choose to say a prayer instead. It is not necessary to do both. You may be drawn to set an intention in one instance and say a prayer in another. Whichever you are called to do is the one you will find most beneficial. Prayer is unique to the individual and influenced by faith and beliefs. You may use this example as a guideline. Then, draw upon personal sentiments and speak from your heart.

Example: "Mother, Father, God, Creator of all that is, I thank you for all of the many blessings in my life. I thank you for this opportunity to heal and for the energy that will flow through me in this process. Please help me in removing all relevant roadblocks and clear my path so that I may _____. I ask that this be done in the now moment for my greater good and the greater good of all humanity. So be it and so it is."

Allowing Creation Energy to Radiate Through

Creation energy is the sum total of all frequencies which are accessible to you, in your creation grid, for the ability to create your life according to your desires. (For more information on grids, see Chapter 10). It is formed in your heart at the intersection of Source Energy coming down from the Creator and Earth energy coming up from the Earth's core. This energy provides the foundation upon which your life and your reality are created. Aligning with Creation Energy will amplify your ability to create in accordance with Divine will. It also increases your ability to transmute obstacles. Though it is always present, it may become stagnated or blocked. Becoming consciously aware of it improves your ability to tune in to all of the activated frequencies, especially those of the highest vibration.

Creation Energy is radiated outward from your heart, through intention. Simply be the channel through which it flows. The energy will begin with a feeling of warmth in the center of your heart chakra. From there it will radiate outwards in all directions until it encompasses your entire being. After a few moments, you will begin to radiate light from the chakras in your fingertips and toes. Send your attention to the presence of the energy, knowing that it is available to you anytime you desire to call upon it.

Opening to Divine Guidance

As creation energy flows through, begin to feel more aware of the spirit that surrounds you. You are supported in every way. You are loved by many. Fill your heart with gratitude for those who have come to help. Understand that this guidance comes through when you are open to receive. Listen to what they have to say. Any messages or instructions they have for you will be received throughout the course of your session. Heed their advice. Thank them for imparting their wisdom.

Assistance

You may choose to connect with specific assistance of Divine origin for support and encouragement throughout your session. If you are governed by a particular faith or religion, you may choose to stay within the confines of that governing. For instance, if you are Protestant, you may be drawn to work with Jesus and the Holy Spirit. If you are Catholic, you may consider calling in the angels and saints, in addition to Jesus. If you are Buddhist, call upon Buddha. If you are Hindu, ask for assistance from Hindu Gods and Goddesses. If you are Muslim, ask Allah to assist you. If you are Native American, call upon the Great Spirit. If you are Pagan, consider asking for help from the Earth, trees, crystals and stones. If you are unsure of faith or religion or are open to higher assistance from all faiths, call upon anyone whose presence expands your heart and raises your vibration. Do what feels comfortable to you. This system was designed for the creation of a heart centered reality that can work within the context of any faith. For more ideas to get you started, take a look at the "Assistance" column on Part I of the Activating Ascension Tools Tables (Appendix C).

Recap of the Opening Sequence: Clear your mind, open your heart and become present. Open the sacred circle and allow a pure connection between self and Source. Come into your sacred heart and state your intention or say your prayer. Radiate creation energy and love and open to receive divine guidance. Connect with your assistance.

Chapter 5, *Agendas, Aspects and Obstacles,* explains how items are grouped together for release. In Chapters 6 and 7 you will learn all of the associated techniques and the closing sequence will be covered in Chapter 8. You now have all you need to begin. As you work with this energy over time, the process will get faster and faster. Your system will resonate in accordance with the energy more and more and you will come into alignment very quickly.

Opening an Activating Ascension Session: Recap

Open Sacred Circle
Establish a Pure Connection
Sacred Heart Connection
Setting of Intention or Opening Prayer
Radiate Creation Energy
Open to Receive Divine Guidance
Connect with Assistance

Melissa

Melissa made her way in to see me through a mutual friend. She was riddled with severe vertigo, unable to focus on her work or her passion for painting. She had regularly seen a physical therapist who had prescribed a strict diet, free from grains and very low in sugar. She was also seeing an acupuncturist and was being treated in accordance with Chinese medicine. From a structural and dietary standpoint, almost everything that could be done, was being done.

When Melissa came in for her first visit, she was unable to lie down due to the vertigo initiated by the change in position. We proceeded with sound therapy through the use of tuning forks, combined with Creation Energy. As our sessions progressed, she was able to lie down. Each time, there was less and less vertigo to contend with and, when it was exacerbated, we were able to shift out of it quickly. She followed the guidance we received with complete trust, even when we took our session outside for navigation of an energy obstacle course to find her true north.

Melissa taught me that emotional experiences trigger physical pain and decreased mobility. She had pain and limited motion in her right shoulder, unassociated with physical trauma. We were able to identify and release each experience being held there and, as each was released, more and more mobility was restored. The pain left and her shoulder range of motion returned to normal. This experience led to the development of Blueprint Restoration and forms a significant piece of what I offer through Holistic Integration.

She attended the retreat as well, took to the protocol instantly and began implementing Activating Ascension into her life immediately. Now, I only see her when she needs a little extra help.

Chapter 4: Agendas, Obstacles, and Aspects

The purpose of this section is to trigger conscious awareness of all blocks to intention, to allow for their comprehensive clearing. Without this trigger, you may not be able to clear as deeply as desired and frustration may arise as you are confronted in the future by agendas you thought had previously been cleared. This process allows the biggest possible picture to be seen, so that you may be fully aware of the multifaceted nature of all that is standing between you and your intention, while mitigating opportunity for frustration and resentment. All of these concepts are explained in detail, below.

Overview: The first step is to intuitively determine the number of agendas that are inhibiting the manifestation of your intention. Next, identify each agenda and the obstacles contributing to their presence. The number of associated aspects is noted, before and after each clearing. After all relevant agendas, obstacles and aspects are identified, you will be ready to clear them with the appropriate techniques. The Activating Ascension Session Guide (Appendix C) is where you will record your intention, the number of agendas, the agendas, obstacles and techniques.

Note: The Activating Ascension Tools Tables (Appendix B) and Session Guide (Appendix C) are available for download on the www.activatingascension.com website.

Agendas

Simply stated, agendas are made up of groups of obstacles. They are labeled intuitively and represent the obstacles to be released for their clearing and for the manifestation of the desired intention. There may be one agenda (or group of obstacles) acting as a barrier to progress, or there may be dozens. Intuitively ask how many agendas are ready to be released. Cast no judgment upon the number, simply make a note of it on the Activating Ascension Session Guide (Appendix C) where it reads "# of Agendas". There is room to clear up to three agendas per Session Guide. Use additional sheets when necessary.

Note: Not all agendas need to be cleared within the context of a single session. For example, there may be seven agendas acting as barriers. You may choose to clear them all at once, a few at a time, or one at a time. It is completely up to you and the pace with which you feel most comfortable.

Now that you are aware of the number of contributing agendas, identify each. For ideas of possible agendas, consult the Activating Ascension Tools Table: Part I (Appendix B). They will be found in the second column, to the right of Assistance. Agendas may represent an undesirable presence, such as that of a particular symptom or a specific fear. They may also represent lack of what is desired, such as wealth or overall happiness. If you receive very clear intuitive guidance as to the name of each of your agendas, you may not need to consult the Tools Table. They are simply suggestions to get you started and help you feel more comfortable with the process. Be as specific as possible in your labeling. For instance, if you are using the Tools Tables and you intuit that there is an agenda of "fear", take it to the next level and find out what specific fear is involved. It is possible to have multiple agendas within one broader category. For example, when dealing with fear, there could be fear of the unknown, fear of rejection and fear of not being enough. Record each type of fear in a separate column.

As each agenda is identified, record it on the Session Guide (Appendix C) on one of the three lines found under Agendas and Corresponding Number of Aspects. Broad categories of agendas include physical symptoms, fear, relationships, career, overall happiness and finances. Miscellaneous possibilities include disconnection from normalcy, the desire to just get by, lack of acceptance, missing the big picture, the need to detach from your story and the need for atonement. The list of possible agendas provided for your consideration on the Tools Table is not comprehensive. However, over 90% of what applies to you will likely fit into the listed categories. Allow conscious awareness of the agendas to rise from heart centered space, for the other 10%.

Once the agendas you will be working with in your session have been identified and recorded, visualize them being filled with Creation Energy, knowing that whatever is keeping this situation from resolution may be transmuted.

 Wade

It was destiny that our paths would cross. Before I moved down to Tennessee, I was introduced to Wade through a social media network. He sent me a message that said, "I could use a chiropractor for a friend." As there was a picture of himself water skiing on his page, I responded with, "I could use a friend that has a boat." Fast forward several months and our paths cross again. I made the move south and within a few months met the man I would marry. He was facilitating a renew group at our church and when I went with him, Wade was sitting at our table. I remember thinking that he looked familiar, but it wasn't until he started talking about skiing that everything clicked.

Wade started coming in for chiropractic care and we became family. I learned about the near death experience he had the previous year while barefoot skiing. It threw his life into a whirlwind that he was having a difficult time recovering from. He decided to attend the retreat and this is what he had to say about it:

"I have always trusted my intuition and been able to feel people's energy. Until recently when a few life events had knocked me off course and caused me to not trust myself. After the Activating Ascension retreat, I literally felt like I had been cured of a disease. I had no idea I was carrying so much stuff around with me for so long. I guess I had categorized it as experience to be held on to for future reference but really it was like a chain around my waist that was dragging me down. The class also gave me many different exercises to do DAILY to help prevent getting off course from my destiny or highest purpose. The exercises I learned in the class, especially the ones dealing with stress, have allowed me to be way more relaxed and made it possible for me to make better choices for my life. In short, any area of your life you think needs improvement can be changed by taking this class and implementing the exercises into your daily routine. Activating Ascension will give you CONTROL of your life or any aspect of it you are struggling with right now, through surrender, and you don't have to wait for the results. You will feel better as soon as you take this class! I promise."

Wade was the designated grounder for the retreat, holding people's feet whenever the energy of the clearings, combined with the higher vibrations of our group consciousness, became challenging to contain within the physical body. Shortly after the initial sequence of retreats, Wade decided to quit his job because he didn't feel good about the work he was being paid to do. This transition came with challenges and bumps in the road, yet he was able to implement the things he learned. Eventually, he moved back to his home state of Florida. He is able to ski to his heart's content and feels good about his employment.

Obstacle Identification

As stated above, groups of obstacles make up an agenda. There may be one obstacle or there may be fifteen for a given agenda. Again, withhold judgment. As with the number of agendas, make a note of the number of obstacles to ensure that each is identified. There is space on the Session Guide (Appendix C) to list each obstacle underneath its associated agenda. If you run out of room, continue on the back. Only use the Session Guide if you find it helpful.

Part II of the Tools Table (Appendix B) is dedicated to obstacles. Possibilities include: emotions, past life issues, experiences, consciousness patterns, triggers, behaviors, inherited beliefs, false mental matrices, completed contracts and a miscellaneous category. Once you have an understanding of the number of obstacles involved with the given agenda, refer to the Tools Table, so that each may be identified. This is not a comprehensive list, though it is designed to serve as a starting point. Your search begins across the columns to find the generalized category and proceeds down the category to identify the specific obstacle. Intuitively ask which generalized category contains your first agenda, beginning with the emotions category. Work your way across the categories until you find the appropriate one. Once the category has been identified, intuitively work your way down the list until you find the obstacle specific to your agenda. Remember to list each obstacle underneath the agenda on the Session Guide.

As with agendas, there may be more than one obstacle within a given category. For example, there may be four obstacles within the emotions category and two within behaviors. Oftentimes, obstacles are revealed in the order of relevance. Do not assume that all obstacles within a given category will be intuitively recognized at the same time. For this reason, begin at the beginning after each obstacle is identified. For example, if the first obstacle you identify is a false mental matrix, search for the second obstacle, at the beginning of the table under the Emotions category.

Most of what you need will be found on this table. If you come to a column and nothing is ringing true, quiet your mind and allow the answer to rise to conscious awareness from your heart center.

Emotions: Any emotion coming from a place of less than love can act as an obstacle to the forward path. Examples include but are not limited to: fear, anger, rage/fury, sadness, depression, disappointment, exhaustion, remorse, guilt, hatred, blame, shame, irritation, frustration, competition, insecurity, jealousy, resentment, annoyance, confusion, anxiety and revenge.

Past Life Blocks: Many faiths believe in reincarnation; that the body is released in death and the spirit born again through reincarnation. No one knows for sure whether or not this is true. Other faiths believe that you only live once and continue on, after death, to eternal life or damnation. Again, no one really knows for sure if this is true. Proponents of both sides passionately believe they are right.

If your religious indoctrination has taught you that you only live in physical form once, you are asked to consider two things. When you take the idea of having multiple incarnations into your heart, how does it feel? Does it resonate as truth when viewed in this context? Secondly, does it really matter if past lives exist or not, if, in clearing them, the obstacle is removed and you are now able to move forward? It may simply be a placebo effect. Either way, do not allow the issue of past lives to deter you from clearing the rest of your obstacles.

Obstacles stemming from past lives could come from a plethora of situations; misuse of power, betrayal, abandonment, religious persecution, or loss of a loved one, to name a few. Unresolved past life experiences may be deeply ingrained into the fiber of your current life. Be gentle with yourself as these come to awareness.

Experiences: Experiences from this life may be holding you back in the same way. They may be traumatic in nature or seemingly inconsequential. Times when you've been caught off guard, accepted other people's beliefs or opinions as truth, or chose the wrong path, are all possible examples. While you cannot go back and change what happened, trust that you can release the experience so as to not relive it each time you think of it.

Consciousness Patterns: A consciousness pattern is a fundamental expression of identity in response to life's circumstances. Its expression happens automatically and you may be so intrinsically attached to it that it becomes your signature role. This is not something that you may be consciously choosing to do. Rather, it evolves out of your subconscious. Examples include: martyr, victim, people pleaser, addict, perfectionist, liar, needy and turned off (unwilling or unable to participate in life).

Triggers: Triggers are behaviors that, when witnessed, elicits an irrational reaction or overreaction. There are three basic reasons why these behaviors have such an effect. They act as a mirror and reflect back to you qualities for which you have judged yourself harshly, either presently or in the past. For example, a reformed liar that has been unable to forgive himself for past mistakes, will be triggered by lies committed by others. Similarly, someone who tends to manipulate others to get what they want will judge other manipulators harshly and be triggered by their behavior.

Secondly, you may be triggered when others are able to express characteristics that you deny to yourself. Consider someone who is ruled by the need to be perfect. They must adhere to strict parameters in hopes of reaching the bar of perfection. These people will be triggered by others who may appear to be sloppy, silly or otherwise out of control, because those are luxuries they would never allow themselves.

Lastly, you may be triggered by the belief systems of others that are contradictory to yours. For instance you may be triggered by homosexuality because it goes against your religious indoctrination. The more available you are to understand the beliefs of others and the more tolerant you are of yourself, the less affected by these triggers you will be. Examples of triggers include: being lied to, manipulated, controlled, judged, looked down upon, rejected, laziness and perceived selfishness. There are an infinite number of possible triggers.

Behaviors: The behavior column pertains to behaviors expressed by you that are contributing to the stagnation of your energy and inhibiting your ability to affect positive change. Behaviors often reflect self sabotage and are directed towards self. Self sabotage is a reaction of the ego when it perceives a desire to move beyond what it believes you are worthy of or deserve. Awareness of the behavior is the first step in their release. Possible behaviors include: being argumentative, controlling, needy, deceitful and inconsiderate.

Inherited Beliefs: These beliefs have been passed down to you directly through avenues of nature, in your DNA, as well as through nurturing from your parents and grandparents, their parents and grandparents and so on. Some beliefs are beneficial and nourish your ability to create. Others represent beliefs of how the world works, evolving out of hardship and difficult times. For instance, if your parents or grandparents grew up in America during the Great Depression, you may have received the inherited belief that life is hard or you can't change your circumstances. Inherited beliefs often evoke ideas of lack and a sense of hopelessness. Other examples include, "you have to work hard to make money", "good things happen to other people" and "you have to do it all by yourself". Review the Tools Table for a more extensive list.

False Mental Matrices: False mental matrices are similar to inherited beliefs, but have evolved directly from your reaction to life experiences. They are false beliefs that shadow your ability to truthfully see yourself, claim your power and successfully create your reality. These are the "I am" statements that relentlessly play in the background of your mind. I am ugly, fat, stupid, not good enough, unworthy, etc. These beliefs convince you that there is not enough, even though the world in which you live is abundant. Further examples include: the belief that everyone is out to get you, the world is bad, scary and dangerous and the situation is doomed anyway. You will find more examples to spark your intuition on the Tools Table.

Completed Contracts: Contracts are agreements you make for the benefit of your spiritual growth and evolution so that you may learn and grow in accordance with your soul's desire, while in physical form. They are made by your higher self and are often agreed to before incarnating, though they may be made during your incarnation. A completed contract will act as an obstacle when you have learned the lesson, but are emotionally unable to let go of the constraints it necessitated. These contracts may be carried over multiple incarnations and may interfere with your ability to learn your next set of lessons.

For example, in a previous life you may have been a monk and taken vows of poverty to assist in a release of materialism and a deepening of your spiritual practice. While your contract was completed in that lifetime, residues of it have continued to affect your ability to create differently in a new life. Holding onto this contract results in the belief that in order to be spiritual you must disavow materialistic endeavors. This worked while you were a monk because you were supported. You didn't have to provide for a family or pay bills. Now, in this new life, you are not supported as such. You have need for income and material goods. However, you find that when money is abundantly flowing, there is an unexpected breakdown of your vehicle, a medical emergency to pay for or you are laid off. These are residual effects of not being able to disconnect from the contract.

For a current life example, consider a completed contract of obedience. Perhaps you were born into a strict family and behavioral expectations of conformity were extremely high. During this time, it was necessary to be obedient, to do as you were told and as was expected. You learned these lessons and were obedient to the best of your ability. Now you are grown, the contract has been completed, but the residual effects are still permeating your life. You find yourself unable to make even the simplest decisions and are always waiting for someone else to tell you what to do. This is a completed contract in need of release.

Other examples of completed contracts include: silence, celibacy, servitude, being less than, resisting divinity, denying mastery and illness. For a more comprehensive list, consult the Tools Table.

Miscellaneous: This group encompasses those obstacles that don't fit into one specific category. They represent errors of interpretation and a veering off of the divine path. They are marked by an inability to allow, receive and/or to reveal your true self. Also included in this group is misunderstanding, misdiagnosis of the problem, the wrong prescription and falling for the illusion.

Aspects

Aspects represent the sum total number of times an agenda has compromised your ability to make the best possible decision, thereby negatively influencing outcomes. This number is intuitively received for each agenda, before and after clearing. On the Session Guide, you will find three sets of parentheses underneath the area where you have written your agendas and three more sets across the bottom where it says "remaining # of aspects". After completion of the recommended techniques (covered in Chapters 5 and 6), you will notice that this number decreases.

Releasing agendas and their associated obstacles, through the techniques outlined in following chapters, allows the energy around each of these decisions to be clarified, balanced and harmonized. It is almost as if you are able to go back in time and shift your perspective of each situation in accordance with the highest good. This does not change the outcome of what happened, though it will influence your reaction and ability to choose differently the next time a decision is to be made in a similar circumstance. For instance, it will help shift the energy around how well you are able to trust, accept and forgive. In this regard, Activating Ascension helps to heal the past, making it easier to move forward.

After obstacle identification, intuitively ask for the number of aspects pertaining to the corresponding agenda. Record the number within the parentheses. After completion of the technique section, intuitively ask again and record the new number. Understand that the new number represents the remaining number of times this agenda has influenced your decision making abilities, still in need of energetic reprocessing. Also, understand that the number of aspects pertains specifically to the agenda and intention with which you are working. In other words, it is not all-inclusive. With every clearing, the door for all that no longer serves to leave through, is opened wider and wider. It is possible, that in clearing significant portions of these aspects, the rest will finish reprocessing autonomously, as the new level of healing is integrated (Chapter 7). It is also possible that you will need to revisit these aspects in your next session, clearing them with additional techniques.

To recap: Agendas are groups of obstacles inhibiting your ability to manifest the desired intention. Aspects represent the influence of the agenda on your perspective. Each of these is to be identified and recorded prior to completion of techniques. The remaining number of aspects is to be recorded afterwards. Consult the Tools Tables and Session Guide to become familiar with the flow.

Chapter 5: Techniques ~ Part I

Eventually, all techniques will become irrelevant as mass consciousness continues to evolve and vibration rises. When able to live completely from your heart and in the moment, there will be no space for obstacles to be stored. They will be instantaneously released as the desire for them to leave arises. Until that time, such techniques exist as constructs for release, repair and rebalance. The premise of Activating Ascension is that conscious awareness of obstacles, as previously discussed, leads to a deeper and more powerful release than would otherwise be possible. The following techniques were intuited for use with the Activating Ascension protocol, though they may be used within the context of other healing systems or independently as part of a daily energy routine. The Part I techniques are simple by design for optimal accessibility and ease of use. They are brief meditations, visualizations and exercises for the intention of releasing obstacles through the creation of flow. Visit www.activatingascension.com for audio/visual descriptions of these techniques. They allow for maximal release and shift of perspective in a short amount of time for situations in and outside of the healing setting. There is great flexibility in how they may be used. Let your intuition be your guide for the greatest benefit.

For use in conjunction with Activating Ascension, intuitively ask to determine how many techniques are recommended for the clearing of a particular agenda and then identify each. Use the Tools Tables: Part I (Appendix B) to assist you. Perform each technique in the order they are identified. Prior to your first Activating Ascension session, read through each of the techniques and become familiar with them. There may be a few you are compelled to complete. Use discernment and only complete those to which you are clearly called.

The techniques of Part I create channels for clearing and release, opening the ego to the possibility of surrender. This section begins with Number Activation Sequences, because they are widely used throughout the system. Techniques to develop intuition, clear confusion within the nervous system and ground your energies follow. Resistance, anger, fear releases and many more techniques will be explored. With practice you will be able to run through these techniques with minimal reference. Until then, refer to their descriptions. Consider choosing a few techniques from Part I and Part II to be used for a daily energy routine. Allow the routine to evolve over time, adding variety, to better serve you on your journey.

Number Activation Sequences

Because many of the Activating Ascension techniques involve predetermined Number Activation Sequences, this will be the first to be discussed. Numbers are extremely powerful and can be used to activate dormant frequencies or deactivate frequencies that no longer serve you. Everything, both tangible and intangible, is energy and all energy vibrates according to its frequency. These frequencies are not separate from you, they are inherently part of you. As your vibration rises, you will be able to activate higher frequencies and deactivate lower ones. This is the basic premise behind any technique, including number activations. Think of these numbers as the combination to a lock within you. When the proper code is entered, the lock is opened and access to the desired frequencies is granted. For example, frequencies of love, joy and happiness may be activated as frequencies of bitterness, anxiety, unforgiveness or shame are deactivated.

Clear your mind, come into your heart and allow a number sequence to rise to conscious awareness. When no more numbers are heard, the sequence is complete. Remember, trying to hear numbers, or trying with any intuitive or energetic technique, only pushes the desired result farther away. This happens when the ego, or mind, is in control. Your ego must be surrendered so that your heart may be a clear channel for the flow of numbers, or other intuitive guidance. You will know the purpose of the numbers based upon the obstacle you are clearing at the time. Do not write them down or try to revisit them.

This technique, and all others, may be used in acute situations when stress levels are elevated. In times such as these, use a Number Activation Sequence for superficial clearing and determine the underlying cause, or obstacle, once you have more clarity and the acuteness of the situation has passed. Then, perform a more thorough clearing.

Intuition Upgrade

A heightened sense of intuition will increase ease of navigation through the Activating Ascension protocol. These techniques may be used in combination with exercises you learned earlier in the Opening Intuition section of this book. Divine guidance is instantaneously available to all who seek it, through intuitive channels. How well this guidance is heard depends on one's ability to listen. The word intuition can be interpreted in several ways. Ultimately, it is an inner knowing of truth and the ability to use that truth. Intuition may be perceived as a gut feeling, communication with your soul-self or guidance from a higher power. All such perceptions are accurate.

The following exercises are designed to assist you in removing any energetic blindfolds, earplugs, earmuffs and the like, preventing you from seeing or hearing the guidance offered through intuitive means. The more often you complete these exercises, the quicker you will notice the improvements. As you work through this system, there may be times when you feel as though you've come up against a wall. Nothing will make sense, your answers will be contradictory, and you will not be able to move forward. Instead of reveling in frustration and irritation, return to these exercises and walk through the doors that will open. You may resonate with one exercise over another. Choose the one that speaks the most to you. After an Intuitive Upgrade technique, complete a five to ten minute journal entry. Allow a stream of consciousness to flow through revealing new understanding of intuitive guidance.

Cloud Messages: Visualize your being floating high above a moonlit sky. Though it is dark, there is more than enough light to clearly see. White, luminescent clouds roll into your awareness from the north. They are friendly and supportive and are here to expand awareness and understanding of that which you perceive to be unclear. The clouds move about, at your request, so that they are floating below you in a semicircle. Fill the clouds with all of your fears, attachments, expectations and resistance. Completely empty yourself of ego. Breathe deeply and release even more. Once the clouds have been filled, an alchemical reaction takes place. The clouds become filled with golden light as transmutation is completed. As energy is moved between them, they expand as deeper perspectives and understandings are

85

unlocked. The ends of the semicircle extend outward towards each other until a continuous circle is formed. Turn yourself so that you are facing the opposite direction, ready to see that which was previously hidden. On an inhale breath, receive into your heart conscious awareness of the alchemical gifts of the clouds. Absorb what they offer. Once complete, the clouds return to the North and you return to your body. Open your eyes and make note of all that was revealed, integrating this higher level of understanding into your being on a cellular level.

Lotus Flower Meditation: Visualize yourself seated inside a lotus flower, fully bloomed. Breathe in its pleasantly sweet smell. Feel comforted by the peacefulness of the water that surrounds you. Breathe the energy of the flower into your heart center. Fill your being with love and gratitude. Allow all frequencies of lack to be transmuted now. Choose serenity. Become aware of the inner knowingness of your sacred heart. Be filled with the power that is innately yours. Repeat this number activation sequence, eight times, to activate frequencies within that will allow you to access more information in regard to your specific questions: **862964818 972165842 691295981**. After the eighth repetition, listen for additional numbers, uniquely for you. Return to conscious awareness after all numbers have been received.

Pink Sphere: While comfortably seated, and in heart-centered space, request a pink sphere of light from the assistance with which you have connected for your session. Breath deeply and allow it to permeate your entire being, freeing any resistance being stored in your cells or light body. Allow it to release all blinders, blindfolds, earplugs, earmuffs and anything else you could be holding that is interfering with your ability to accurately interpret and understand your current situation from the highest possible perspective. Use the pink sphere of light to clear and transmute all cobwebs surrounding an issue and making it difficult for you to see the answers clearly. Once the cobwebs have been cleared, claim your answers.

Creation of Intuitive Flow through Movement: Resistance to truth causes a stagnation of energy in the physical being. Complete this exercise to release the resistance and stagnation so that flow may be created. Stand tall, feet shoulder width apart, hands on your hips. Tilt your head slightly upward. Rotate your upper body clockwise, engaging your entire body to make five circles as large as you comfortably can. Repeat in the opposite direction. Energetically clear emotional sleepiness and fatigue from your eyes and wash your hands of attachment. Allow your spirit to be invigorated and be willing to see the highest truth.

 Emily

Emily came in as a referral from her Aunt. She was one of the first patients I had as the foundation for Activating Ascension was being formed. I still remember handing her the brochure for the very first retreat I offered (following guidance to share it with everyone without much faith that anyone would be interested). Emily looked at the brochure with intrigue and said she felt like it was something she really wanted to do. I am grateful for the wonderful friendship that has grown out of those initial exchanges.

As most do, Emily was struggling to find herself in her marriage and in her career. She was looking for her voice and her place - how to be married without losing herself and how to be employed in the corporate world without going insane. She attended the retreat and her inner healer began to awaken. Over the last two years, she has found herself in her marriage and is about to find

87

herself in the relationship between a mother and a child. Emily is completing her transition out of a high-stress career and into a healing ministry, incorporating everything she has learned through studies in nutrition, herbology, personal training, Reiki, Activating Ascension and her ordainment in the Order of Melchizedek. She is proving the falsity of the old paradigm and helping to pave the way for the emergence of the new. To learn more about Emily's work, please visit www.reverendemily.com.

Switching

If you are having difficulty receiving clear and consistent answers you may be what is commonly called "switched". Think of this phenomenon as confusion within your autonomic nervous system. Explanation of switching is presented below, followed by techniques to assist you in the release of any such confusion so that you may move forward with clarity.

Your autonomic nervous system is divided into two parts: the sympathetic and parasympathetic nervous systems. Autonomic means to function autonomously, as this system needs no instruction from your brain or central nervous system. It controls functions such as heart rate, blood pressure, digestion, dilation or constriction of pupils, and rate of healing. The sympathetic system is responsible for the "fight or flight" mechanism, while the parasympathetic system oversees "rest and digest". When you are awake and moving about, your sympathetic nervous system should be slightly dominant and when you are asleep, your parasympathetic nervous system should be slightly dominant. When you are switched, the opposite is true.

For example, have you ever gone to bed extremely tired and yet, were unable to sleep? Then, in the morning, when it was time to get up, you were still extremely tired? Fear, excitement, anxiety and other emotions contribute to the expression of switching. The following techniques serve to alleviate the confusion and clear the emotional causes. They shift the internal environment so that these emotions cannot be stored in such a way. Choose the one that resonates most with you.

Heartbeat Harmonization: The Earth emits an energetic impulse and beats rhythmically, similarly to how your heart beats. Close your eyes and use the power of a golden infinity symbol to connect you to the Earth. Visualize yourself in one loop and the Earth in the other. With your breath, allow this energetic connection to strengthen, moving throughout the infinity symbol and balancing in one direction, followed by the other. Feel your heartbeat harmonizing with the Earth. Place your right hand over your right ear and your left hand over your left hip. Take five deep breaths focusing on the crossover of energy from your right hand to your left hand. Once you feel that energy stabilize reverse your hands and repeat. Place both hands on your heart and visualize your entire being filled with a brilliant orange light. Breath deeply for a few moments more and open your eyes when this feels complete.

Cycle the Energy: Sit comfortably with your feet on the floor and your hands in your lap, opened upwards. Energetically wrap your hands, feet and head in the colors of unconditional love, as you perceive them. Allow this colored light of love to move through your being in the following sequence. Begin sending this energy from the right side of your head to your left hand to your right foot. From your right foot, send the energy up to the left side of your head to your right hand to your left foot. Return it to where it began, at the right side of your head. Continue in this direction until the energy flows smoothly and then reverse the order. In this sequence, the energy still begins at the right side of your head, but then flows to your left foot, right hand, left side of your head, right foot, left hand and back to the right side of your head. Following the sequence may seem challenging at first. Continue until the pattern has been fully integrated and it happens without thinking about it.

Red and Blue Make Purple: This exercise reinforces the energetic crossover of information from the right side of your brain to the left side of your body and vice versa. It assists in clearing the confusion associated with being switched while also improving coordination and balance between the rational and creative minds.

Begin seated, feet shoulder width apart and arms down at your sides. Imagine the color red flowing from the right side of your head and down the left side of your body, crossing over at your chin. Once a steady stream of red is flowing, begin imagining the color blue flowing from the left side of your head down the right side of your body simultaneously crossing in the same place. Focus on where the streams of color cross at your chin. Keep imagining the colors until they turn purple at the point of intersection. When the purple appears, the exercise is complete.

Adrenal Connection: The energetic milieu of your adrenals may hold the sympathetic portion of your autonomic nervous system in an over-stimulated state and be a contributing factor in fatigue or exhaustion. This issue is complicated and multifaceted, though this exercise is a wonderful place to begin. The adrenals are small glands that sit just above your kidneys and just below your ribcage on the posterior compartment of your torso. Focus your attention there, filling them with the energy of white roses. Breathe deeply and begin sending this energy outwards in a figure eight pattern, connecting your adrenal glands together within the infinity symbol. Once you feel a shift in one direction, reverse the pattern until a sense of completion is felt.

Grounding

Human beings used to walk the earth with bare feet (or leather bound shoes), be in communion with nature while performing their daily work, and sleep on or near the ground, under the stars. Technological advances of recent times offer conveniences, accompanied by unanticipated side-effects. Rubber-soled shoes now cushion the path and protect feet against injury. Modernization has taken society inside factories and office buildings and created dependence on interaction with computers, wireless connections and cell phones. Even play time is dominated by televisions, movies and video games. Unconsciously, humans are forgetting the importance of their relationship with nature. This is resulting in detrimental changes in genetic patterning, gene expression and evolution that hasn't yet been scientifically studied and recorded. With all its benefits, technology is eroding personal relationships as couples and families sit at the dinner table, mesmerized by the television or caught up in social media on their electronic devices. People are forgetting how to interact with each other on a personal level. Many are isolated and deprived of the human touch they innately desire.

Grounding is the process of anchoring your soul into your physical body through interaction with nature, human touch or intention. It is something that happens naturally when allowed. Interference to grounding is predominantly due to lifestyle changes discussed above. There may also be a lack of intention to be energetically grounded in physical form. You may unconsciously choose to dissociate from your body in attempts to escape from pain, both emotional and physical. Whether it's a disease process, an abusive relationship or feeling as though life on the Earthly plane is simply too hard, there is temptation to live outside the body when the ego's false interpretation is that you are not safe. This will actually lead to an inability to focus or be present and to short-circuiting of your nervous system. On the other end of the spectrum, desiring a spiritual experience and the bliss of being in a meditative state can also cause an imbalance in ability and intention to ground one's soul in physical form. While you are a spiritual being having a physical experience, it is not sustainable to attempt to live outside of your body in the etheric realm. One of the purposes of being born in physical form is to find balance between fulfillment in physical expression and remembrance of the infinite nature of your soul. Committing to be grounded in your body, as a tree is grounded in its roots, is imperative.

While the following techniques will not take the place of communion with nature or human touch, they will give form to intention. If at any time during your Activating Ascension sessions you feel as though you are unable to concentrate and be fully present, consider completing one of these. When possible, do the exercise outside. Use these techniques in everyday life before perceived stressful experiences like important meetings, publicly speaking, tests, interviews and more. They will help limit the physiologic response to stress initiated by your adrenals and associated with these events.

Hands to Earth: This exercise grounds your energy into the Earth. Begin by standing with feet shoulder width apart, knees soft. Breathe in and raise your arms overhead, palms joining in prayer. Exhale and lower your arms down and out at a 45 degree angle, with palms parallel to the floor. On an inhale breath, circle arms to the sides and behind. As you exhale scoop your arms in towards your sides and squat down. Pay attention that your knees do not extend past your toes and that your heels are firmly planted. Come down only as far as you are comfortably able. Visualize streams of energy flowing out of your palms, connecting and anchoring into the center of the earth. Stay here for three deep breaths. Inhale and reverse the movement, bringing palms back overhead in prayer and then lower your arms in front. Repeat three times.

White Light: This exercise grounds the Earth's energy into you. Sit comfortably, feet on the floor, palms facing upward in your lap. Visualize 8 streams of white light coming into your heart from the heart of the Earth. Absorb this white light into your heart center. Send it out to every cell of your being with each beat of your heart. Allow the light to expand with every breath. Once the light fills your physical body, the Earth's energy is fully grounded in you.

Releasing Interference: Use this technique when feeling resistant to being grounded into physical form by anchoring all interference into the Earth for transmutation. Sit comfortably, feet firmly planted, palms up and open in your lap. Use a sieve, however you imagine it to be, to filter out all frequencies of interference. Begin at your crown, pulling the filter through your entire being, channeling all such frequencies into and out of your feet. Allow this energy to flow out of your body and into the Earth from your feet. Through intention, all energy going into the Earth is completely transmuted into pure and unconditional love. Repeat until you feel as though your energy has been grounded and balanced.

Third Eye Clearing: The focus of this technique is to clear energetic excesses of physic residue. All knowledge is available through energetic exchange in the ethers. The answers truly are blowing in the wind. There may be times when your third eye becomes overloaded with too much information. Complete this exercise when you have tapped into frequencies that are not in your highest and best to integrate. Sit comfortably with your feet on the floor, hands in your lap and palms facing up. With eyes open or closed, bring your attention to your third eye, located between and slightly above, your eyebrows. Send out all excess energy through your third eye and watch as it is transformed into pure light. Ask that this light be offered to any and all who may claim and benefit from it.

Resistance

Resistance is defined as a force that tends to oppose or retard motion. With regards to use of the term in this context, resistance is the metaphorical mud that your feet occasionally become mired in on your path to healing and alignment with divine plan. It is your ego causing complete stagnation of your ability to move forward and see things from the highest perspective. Simply put, it's what holds you back. Resistance to the lesson offered will bind your energy and stop you from moving forward. Open yourself to the lesson and allow truth to be revealed. Release the resistance and move forward. Use these techniques to free yourself from the mud. It is helpful to have conscious awareness of what is specifically being resisted. For example, are you resisting love, forgiveness, acceptance, etc.?

Resistance Shake: This is a great exercise to rid yourself of resistance and move your body. Complete a full-body shake for at least one minute to release resistance being stored within your muscles on a cellular level. Do this while standing, if possible, and make sure to move your entire body. Shaking out resistance will lift your spirits and your mood and is a wonderful way to start the day.

Infinity Resistance Release: If you can't get up and shake, use this exercise for release. Visuallze an infinity symbol made of silver and gold light. Place yourself in one loop of the symbol and whatever is being resisted in the other. Allow the silver and gold light to flow around you and your resistance within the infinity symbol, simultaneously in both directions. Do this for at least one minute. If you are unsure of the lesson, simply state your intention that whatever it is you are resisting, be placed in the loop.

Fear

Fear is the foundation upon which all obstacles are built. In any moment, there exists two choices. You may either choose love and peacefully create on faith and truth, or you may succumb to fear, allowing it to shadow your experience, taint your perception and diminish your power. Fear underlies every other emotion of low vibration. It is found lurking beneath the surface of anger, resentment, jealousy, revenge and more. When facing such circumstances, willingness to look within and ask "What am I afraid of?", will calm the ego and allow a deeper understanding. Once the fear has been identified, it can be released. Use this technique to free yourself from fear and build instead upon a foundation of love.

Fear Release: Place your right hand over your spleen. Your spleen is tucked up under the outer aspect of your left rib cage. Place your thumb and ring finger of your left hand together, tip to tip. Take five deep breaths in through your nose and out through your mouth. Stay here until you feel warmth radiating out of your right hand and into your spleen, or otherwise sense completion. Place your left hand over your liver while placing your thumb and ring finger of your right hand together, tip to tip. Your liver is located under the front of your right rib cage. Take five deep breaths in through your nose and out through your mouth. Stay here until you feel warmth radiating out of your left hand and into your liver or otherwise sense completion. Repeat until your perspective has shifted.

95

Love

Love has the power to heal all wounds. Self love is strengthened and fortified through a personal relationship with a Divine Creator and ripples outwardly from within. For some, this relationship is as natural as breathing. For others, it may be more difficult. For all, it is possible. To develop this relationship, consider sitting quietly in silent meditation. Listen for the still, small voice within and know that you are one with this Creator. This connection is understood as it is allowed and cannot be forced. In other words, the more you try, the farther away it is pushed. Lack of self love is recognized by difficulty in sharing unconditional love with others. You cannot fully give something to someone else that you have not fully given to yourself. Love is the guiding force that will see you and your world through challenging times. Divine and Earthly love are available in infinite supply.

Healing with Love: This is a simple technique that allows a great deal of clearing to take place in a short amount of time. Begin by sitting or lying comfortably and peacefully. Close your eyes and allow Source to pour unconditional love down through your crown chakra and into your heart. Allow the center of the Earth to channel unconditional love up through your feet and into your heart. As the power of Divine love merges with the power of Earthly love, allow this energy to be woven throughout your physical body, clearing out any cobwebs and releasing all that no longer serves. Allow as much time as needed and open your eyes when you've felt a shift and feel as though you have cleared as much as possible in the moment.

Anger

Anger is a valid emotion, and you are entitled to it. It can inspire positive change and serve as a motivational call to action. When improperly processed in unbeneficial ways it may be problematic. Suppression of anger or channeling of it into low vibrational paths of expression causes an overreaction of your sympathetic nervous system resulting in decreased immunity, high blood pressure, decreased blood flow to your brain and increased heart rate. This is especially true in cases of chronic anger held over long periods of times. In these instances, whenever you tell your story or reflect on experiences that you have reacted angrily towards, your body re-lives them over and over again causing the same cascade of physiologic events. To your body, it's as if the experience is happening again in the current moment. Anger that is suppressed may result in actions causing harm to yourself or others that will likely be regretted.

Consider the reasons why you are angry, for they are rarely what they appear from a superficial perspective. With a second glance, you may trace your anger back to a decision or mistake of your doing. Often, these are due to miscommunication or absence of attention. It is easier to place blame outwardly than to accept the role you played and forgive yourself for the mistake. Remember that anger is built upon a foundation of fear. Reflect upon the relationship between relevant fears you may have been holding and the events and circumstances that triggered your anger. These sentiments often apply to those situations where you had opportunity to affect a different outcome. There are certainly occasions where there is no opportunity, as in the case of child abuse, war, government suppression, etc.

A considerable amount of energy is required to hold onto anger and the experiences associated with it. If you have stored anger in relation to past events or present circumstances, it's time to release it. Accept the lesson, learn from it and decide to move on in a heart-centered way. Imagine how you could productively employ the energy freed upon release of the anger.

Anger Release: Breathe deeply and visualize where in, or around, your body these emotions are being stored. Allow conscious awareness of all details surrounding the source of the anger and the reasons for its storage to rise. While in heart-centered space, be open to receive a symbolic picture of the emotion. For example, you may see a shaking fist, a red face or a raging bull. Trust the image that you receive and focus your intention there. Say the following number activation sequence five times: **897621 579812 279165 872369**. If additional numbers are given to you at the end of each sequence, say them as well. Pay attention to how the visualization changes after each repetition. As you say the numbers, the symbolic representation of your anger will begin to fade away as anger is released from your physical and energetic beings. Once anger has been released, identify all associated fears and follow this exercise with the Fear Release exercise.

Breathe

The first physiological response to stress is a decrease of lung expansion resulting in shallow breathing. There is much wisdom in the encouragement to breathe. Many people stay so long in a stressed state that they don't even realize they are barely breathing enough to sustain life. They are in survival mode, unable to see the possibility of thriving. Conscious awareness of breath and the intention to breathe fully and deeply are two of the many benefits of yoga and meditative practices. Breathing deeply stops progression of the stress response. The following release technique is simple and readily available whenever you are feeling overwhelmed. You can use it in traffic, before or after confrontation and when faced with a difficult decision. Use it to turn off the stress response, soothe your sympathetic nervous system and encourage an increase in parasympathetic dominance.

Release with Breath: Set your intention to breathe in love, compassion, peace, acceptance, or courage and breathe out fear, shame, sadness, anger or whatever emotion with which you are overcome. Breathe deeply and consciously for three minutes. Release slowly and steadily until the feeling of being overwhelmed has left.

Prayer

Many of the Activating Ascension techniques are based on meditations and visualizations. These exercises require an inner quietness and willingness to listen. Prayer is a way of asking for what you want, through a personal relationship with a Divine Creator. Perhaps you have been petitioning in prayer all your life. Perhaps this will be your first experience. Focus less on the words that form your prayer, and more on the feeling or energy behind the words. To put it another way, there is to be congruence between the words you say and your heart's desire.

Prayer is personal and its expression as unique as the person praying. A loving Creator is a common thread among religions. For universal accessibility, this loving Creator is called "Source" in the context of Activating Ascension. You may replace "Source" with the name that resonates most with you.

Use this technique within a healing session to release agendas and obstacles. Use it in everyday life to raise the vibration of your food, to give thanks, for the petition of your needs and to hold others in the highest light. When praying for others, remember to pray for their highest good in respect to their life path.

Releasing through Prayer: Focus your attention on the obstacles you would like to release. Pay attention to where they are being held. While mentally reviewing them, are particular areas of your physical being triggered? Pain, achiness or sudden awareness of stiffness may indicate areas where obstacles have become imbedded. Other sensations may also act as indicators. If no awareness is experienced, it could be that they are being stored in your auric field, rather than in your physical body. Where in your field can you feel, or otherwise identify, them? You may be guided to use the technique in conjunction with color, shape, sound or a resistance release exercise. Follow your guidance accordingly, remembering that Higher Power can only transmute that which you are willing to release.

Say your prayer and as you do so, intentionally release obstacles from your physical body or auric field. As you feel them release, imagine each piece being placed into a bubble. When you feel as though as many pieces as possible have been released and enclosed in bubbles, visualize each of them coming together in front of your heart center and merging into one. Release the bubble up to Source, knowing that the lessons held in the bubble have been learned and never need be created again.

Breathe deeply for a few minutes after your prayer to continue releasing resistance and to claim freedom from the bubble and all it represented.

Movement

Movement is a great way to release all that no longer serves and to ground a higher vibration and new level of consciousness into your being on a cellular level. The next time you're around children, notice how joyfully and freely they move. Watch as they express themselves naturally and without internal censorship. Think back to when you were a child and the motions and movements that brought you the greatest joy. Were you an excellent hula-hooper? Did you love the wind in your face while cruising the neighborhood streets on your bicycle? Call upon the innocence of youth for inspiration and get moving.

Releasing with Movement: Get up (if you are able), release ego and move your body in accordance with your heart-led inner child. Dance, jump, hop, sway, swing, wiggle. Move in such a way that you are filled with freedom, joy and are energetically recharged. Complete this exercise for five minutes, stopping only when a shift in perspective and higher consciousness is felt.

Use this technique in the grocery store and dance your way down the aisles. Lighten your mood and dance in your seat while at a red light. Hop on one foot to get the morning paper or the afternoon mail. Share your playful side with others and inspire them to move too.

Sound

Human form is fundamentally composed of sound and light. This is why listening to your favorite song or wearing your favorite color helps to decrease your stress level, alter brain chemistry and improve mood, ability to focus and motivation for positive self expression. Music from a happy childhood, when heard as an adult, will fill your thoughts with wonderful memories. The comforting sound of a loved one's voice softens the blow of hurt feelings or the pain of loss. Chanting and toning helps to awaken inner truths and reveal what was before hidden. Sound has the ability to raise vibration, thereby creating the space for release of all that no longer serves your highest good.

Releasing with Sound: There are many possibilities for releasing with sound. Follow your intuition and go with the form that resonates the highest, rather than what feels good. Hold your intention and allow the clearing to flow naturally. Song, instrumental music, drumming, singing bowls, chanting or toning, guttural sounds or tuning forks are some ideas to get you started. Make or listen to the sound until you feel a release, shift or sense of completion. Difficulty using your voice for expression indicates disharmony within your throat chakra and a decreased ability to speak your truth. Practice using your voice, softly at first, then allow it to rise with confidence.

Color

As mentioned earlier color or light, is a fundamental element of living beings. The visible spectrum of light waves includes every color of the rainbow: Red, Orange, Yellow, Green, Blue, Indigo and Violet. Color has the ability to soothe your nervous system similarly to sound. Each color elicits a physiological response when you look at it. Marketing schemes, wall color and lighting are all designed to bring about a desired emotional reaction. The desired emotional response in accordance with Activating Ascension is to create a healing environment for the release of obstacles. Color may be visualized or felt, depending on your intuitive strengths. Some have the ability to visualize color, while others have a sense of knowing or are able to "feel" color. Releasing with color may be used regardless of whether you visualize or feel color.

Releasing with Color: This is a simple technique that is easily accessible in most situations. Sit quietly, close your eyes and breathe deeply. Consider the agenda, obstacle or irritation you would like to clear. While holding this intention, allow awareness of color to flow from your heart. Infuse your intention with this color, watching as it moves through your being, merges with other colors, or contracts and expands. You may see or feel one color, or there may be multiple colors to assist in your clearing. Do not control its path, only observe. This technique is complete when the perception of color fades from conscious awareness.

If you do not perceive through visualization or feeling color flowing from your heart, call to mind an intensely colored rainbow. Meditate on each color for a moment or two and then return to the color to which you had the strongest emotional reaction. Invite that color into your heart and perfuse your intention with it. Allow it to move through your body and watch as it shifts and changes. When it feels as though the energy has stabilized or you are unable to sense the colors presence, the technique is complete.

Shape

Connecting with shapes, and other symbols, amplifies the power of your intention for release. This is not a study in sacred geometry, though there is much to be learned from that field. Reference the Suggested Reading list to explore further.

Releasing with Shape: Typical shapes used in clearing include spheres, squares, pyramids, diamonds, pentagons, and trapezoids. Allow conscious awareness of the most beneficial shapes to rise from heart-centered space. Listen for the location of an obstacle within your physical body or field. Once you have a clear sense of its presence, visualize it being surrounded by the shape. It may remain still or begin to rotate. It may even multiply itself and move into additional areas. Allow the clearing to unfold. Visualize the shapes until you feel a shift or release.

Note: The use of shape is not limited to geometrical patterns. Trust the images as they are revealed, knowing they are exactly what is required for your clearing. You may feel called to connect with flowers, animals, mountains, stars, streams and other representatives of nature's beauty, or objects of sentimental value or emotional connection may materialize. For example, you may connect with a grandmother's love through a vision of a family heirloom.

To Recap: This completes the descriptions for Part I Techniques. Read through them until familiarity is gained and you are able to complete them without reference. Consider integrating two or three of them into a daily energy routine to optimize heart-centered creation. Descriptions for Part II Techniques are found in the following chapter.

 Jo Ann

Jo Ann's experience is a testimony to the profound power of seemingly simple techniques - color, shape, number activations and grounding. When she called in the afternoon, she was extremely distraught. She was crying and her breathing was uneven, like it was hard for her to take a breath. It was the anniversary of a traumatic life event and Jo Ann was overwhelmed with emotion.

As she began telling me about what she was thinking and feeling, I began guiding her through color and shape visualizations and number activation sequences. Guidance was flowing forth quickly and she asked if it mattered whether or not she could keep up with the visualizations. I told her to simply focus on allowing and her subconscious would take care of the color and shape placement. We were on the phone for about twenty minutes when I told Jo Ann to go and sit by a tree, with her back against the trunk and the intention to merge energy fields and ground her feet as though they were the roots of the tree. I trusted the guidance that we had been given and we disconnected.

I received this email response from her the next day: *"I feel soooo much better. There is something powerful in what you did for me. I would like to learn more about it. I feel happier, lighter, and more open to my more optimistic self. I think you must have done some special work on me. THANK YOU. I see you as a mentor and friend. Thank you so much. I love you."*

Chapter 6: Techniques ~ Part II

These techniques require more focus and concentration than the those described in Part I. They may also be found in audio/visual format at www.activatingascension.com. You will find it beneficial to complete the opening sequence for a session before using them, until you are able to come into heart-centered space through intention alone. Part II techniques allow you to move beyond the superficiality of resistance, emotional disturbance and other tricks of the ego. As the ego is surrendered, the possibility for true healing is created. These techniques are presented and described in order of intensive progression. Read them first and as you are learning and becoming familiar with them, only complete those to which you are clearly called. Allow one technique to fully process before continuing to the next. With repetition of these techniques, you will come closer and closer into balance, as small shifts in perspective accumulate to create quantum shifts in consciousness. Their usage within the context of an Activating Ascension session will be intuitively determined. The *Techniques* column of the Tools Table will serve as a reference guide to get you started.

Nervous System Balancing

Your nervous system will respond to conscious commands and instructions. Completing these exercises will create an environment for its optimal functioning and will assist in the integration of new understandings and perspectives. As higher frequencies of consciousness are activated and lower frequencies deactivated, your vibrational range elevates. The shedding of lower vibrations may result in dissonance or irritation within your nervous system. This may lead you to feel as though your "nerves are shot" or that your circuits have been overloaded. The following sets of instructions will correct any such feelings.

There are three sets: Neuronal Balancing and Optimization, Endocrine and Autonomic Nervous System Balancing and Balancing the Yin and Yang. You may come across words that are unfamiliar to you pertaining to the specifics of your anatomy and physiology. Basic definitions and explanations are offered to allow for conscious awareness, though it is not necessary to become thoroughly versed in your understanding of them for the instruction to be given. Remember, energy follows intention. Intend that these instructions create a state of balance and an energetic collaboration will take place to elicit the desired result. Complete one or more of the following instructions.

Note: These techniques are used to clear energetic disturbances before the manifestation of disease. They are not intended to treat medical conditions and are never to be used in place of medical treatment.

Neuronal Balancing and Optimization

This balancing technique pertains to the central nervous system which includes your brain, spinal cord and cranial nerves. Completion of this exercise will facilitate and encourage flow within this system. It will improve the crossover of information between the hemispheres of the brain, leading to a heightened awareness of reality, critical thought development, and the ability to experience life in the moment, free of bias, attachment and expectation.

You may be unfamiliar with some of the terminology used in this instruction. Definitions will be provided here and a basic conscious understanding of them will improve your ability to elicit the desired response. A synaptic junction is the environmental area between cells where communication takes place. The dorsal root ganglion is a communication center on your spinal cord that assimilates information coming from your body and sends it the appropriate receiver in your brain. The prefrontal cortices are the anterior portions of your frontal brain, where thoughts and behaviors are coordinated and orchestrated for the manifestation of your goals and desires. Microglial cells collect toxins and cellular wastes, playing a significant role in central nervous system immunity. Phagocytic describes cells that clear wastes through ingestion. Astrocytes are cells that help protect the blood brain barrier and help regulate ionic concentrations. They also play a role in repair and healing within the nervous system after trauma.

To Begin: Listen for a personalized number activation sequence, infusing the numbers with the intention to establish optimal balance. Visualize yourself in the threshold of a purple doorway, facing forward. Allow violet-white light to pour into your heart, expanding outward in all directions. Connect with your assistance to receive unseen support. Give the following instruction: **"I now**

command that the synaptic junctions of the dorsal root ganglion and the prefrontal cortex be adjusted for optimal functioning. I command the microglial cells to maximize their phagocytic activity. I command the astrocytes to improve their performance of support, protecting the blood brain barrier and control of ionic concentrations, in accordance with my highest good. Let it be done with ease and grace in the now moment. "Visualize stepping through the doorway and into balance.

Endocrine and Autonomic Nervous System Balancing

Your endocrine system is comprised of all of the glands in your body that secrete hormones directly into your bloodstream. This includes the hypothalamus, pineal body, pituitary, thyroid, those of the alimentary system (stomach, duodenum, liver and pancreas), kidneys, adrenals, glands of reproduction (testes, ovaries and, when pregnant, the uterus and placenta), parathyroid and skin. When this system is challenged, energetic patterns are disrupted and communication through feedback loops is distorted. This may lead to a hormonal imbalance and the manifestation of associated symptoms.

Your autonomic nervous system consists of your parasympathetic nervous system (rest and digest), sympathetic nervous system (fight or flight) and sensory and motor neurons. This system functions autonomously, meaning without conscious awareness, to regulate heart rate, blood pressure, vascular dilation, rate of respiration and more. When this system is not functioning optimally, it may be due to an overload of stress for which the parasympathetic nervous system is unable to adequately compensate.

For the purpose of Activating Ascension and the desire to return to a harmonious state, focus is placed upon the adrenals (for regulation of stress), heart complex (for regulation of the circulatory system, including heart rate and blood pressure), pancreas (for regulation of insulin and digestive processes), the renin-angiotensin cascade (for further regulation of blood pressure as affected by the kidneys and lungs), and the reproductive system. As energetic balance is returned within these components, the space is created for all other components to come into balance.

To Begin: Intuitively ask which of the above components are in need of balancing. Listen for a personalized number activation sequence, backed by your intention to balance these systems. Visualize yourself surrounded in a green oval, with golden light radiating outward from its center. Allow those who have come to assist to provide unseen support. Give the following instruction: **"I now command that my _____ automatically normalize and that all energetic connections and supports, within and without, be repaired to bring my endocrine and autonomic nervous systems into perfect balance and harmony in the now moment."** This is complete when the golden light expands beyond the green oval.

Balancing the Yin and Yang

Yin and yang are philosophical concepts central to Chinese sciences, traditional Chinese medicine and Chinese martial arts. They are representative of the nature of duality and polarity, interconnection and interdependence. They are intrinsically interrelated and interwoven. These forces are complementary to each other and necessary to create a whole greater than its parts. In other words, one cannot exist without the other (as in the case of the two sides of a coin). Yin energies are characterized as feminine in nature, while yang energies are associated with masculinity. Completing this exercise will help to bring the masculine and feminine components of your being into perfect balance. The harmonious interactions of the two will help bring clarity in the face of difficult decisions, allowing for a greater understanding of all perspectives and the ability to proceed in the highest possible way.

To Begin: Listen for a personalized number activation sequence, while holding the intention of restoring the balance. Visualize yourself surrounded by a pink, three dimensional star of David, with silver light emanating outwards, in all directions, from the center. Allow those who have came to assist to provide unseen support. Give the instruction: **"I now command that the natural interconnections and interdependence of the yin and yang energies, intrinsic to every cell in my being, be optimized and elevated to the most beneficial balance."** Balance is attained when the silver light expands beyond the Star of David.

Energetic Remedies

Since everything is energy and all energy vibrates at a frequency, the vibrational effect of all things is available to you in physical and energetic form. Meaning, it is possible to "download" and integrate the frequency of that which is desired, through intention. As your vibration increases, so will your ability to download frequencies. This can be done for emotions (peace, love, acceptance, etc.) as well as supplements and homeopathic remedies (to provide physical support for your intentions). The clearer you are as a channel, the more likely you will be able to integrate these frequencies without their physical presence.

Supplements and homeopathic remedies have many benefits. They assist in the healing process by providing raw materials for the body. As you are guided to this technique, intuitively ask if you would benefit from a supplement, homeopathic remedy or both. It is possible that you will be guided to one or more of each. Possible supplements are listed below to get you started. Homeopathic remedies follow. Complete the instructions for each, allowing them to fully process before continuing. You will know if the physical presence of that which has been energetically downloaded is required, based upon your recommended follow up (Chapter 8).

Dietary Supplements
Dietary supplements help to make up the difference between nutrient consumption in food and nutrients required by the body. Possibilities include: Vitamins, minerals, trace minerals, omega 3 fatty acids, Coenzyme Q10, protomorphogens, probiotics. Vitamins are organic compounds and minerals are inorganic compounds. Both provide necessary nutrients for health. Trace minerals are minerals required in small amounts. Omega 3 fatty acids are vital to cell metabolism and support the heart, brain and a plethora of bodily processes. Coenzyme Q10 plays a vital role in energy production and also works as an antioxidant, thereby inhibiting free radical formation and the damage they cause. Protomorphogens are cellular secretions that support protein synthesis and cell repair and play a role in immunity. Probiotics help to establish beneficial levels of gut bacteria for healthy digestion and elimination. For this purpose, the general category ("vitamins" or "minerals") is specific enough. Working within the broader category will affect the balance and coordination of the specific components within it.

To Begin: Open to receive and ask for support from your assistance. Clearly state your intention for frequency download by offering the following: **"I open myself to receive the perfect combination of _____ to bring my system into optimum balance and functioning. I am open to receive it in a steady stream, for as long as it is in my highest and best."**

While the download completes, place one hand on your heart and the other hand on your sacral chakra, below your belly button. Breathe deeply and use color or sound to release any resistance that my rise to the incoming frequencies. Allow the download, and its integration, to fully complete before continuing.

Homeopathy
Homeopathy is based on the premise that "like cures like". In simplest terms, this means that what makes you sick, when diluted down numerous times, will spark a response within your immune system to make you better. Consider the intention you have stated for your session and use the following exercise to download the highest and most beneficial homeopathic remedy to assist you in its manifestation.

To Begin: Open to receive and ask for support from your assistance. Focus awareness on your intention and offer the following: **"I am open to receive the most beneficial homeopathic remedies to assist me in _____. I am open to receive it in the most beneficial concentration, in a steady stream for as long as it is in my highest and best."**
While the download completes, place one hand on your heart and the other hand on your sacral chakra, below your belly button. Breathe deeply and use color or sound to release any resistance that my rise to the incoming frequencies. Allow the download and its integration to fully complete before continuing.

Cords

For the creation of a heart-centered reality, all connections to self and to others are to be cultivated from a place of love. Connections with others from a place of less than love can result in the unconscious sending or reception of energetic threads, cords or tentacles. These cords typically come and go from your solar plexus, located in your belly, though it is possible for them to be sent or received from anywhere in your field. If you have an awareness of someone pulling on your energy field or if you feel drained, exhausted or saddened after talking with or being around certain people, it is possible that they have corded into you, and likely you have corded into them as well. These cords are easily discerned when coming to or from those who trigger you in some way and whose company is typically avoided. They are slightly more difficult to discern when coming to or from those for whom you deeply care. Remember that worry, fear and doubt all originate from vibrations less than love. Establishment of a heart-to-heart connection between you and a higher power creates the space within you to share that same heart-to-heart connection with all others. Set your intention to stay in heart-centered space and share only love. With conscious awareness and practice, you will find it to be your natural state. Until then, use the following technique to release all cords and establish heart-to-heart connections.

Note: The cords that hold you bound in less than beneficial ways to others may also hold you bound to experiences, places, ages and objects. Releasing these cords makes it easier to release the past and come into the present with love.

Cord Release: Visualize your entire being surrounded by an aquamarine crystal pyramid. Create a silver thread of light growing out of the top of the pyramid and anchoring into the heart of your

Higher Power. Create a silver thread of light growing out of the bottom of the pyramid and anchoring into the center of the Earth. Visualize all energetic cords, threads or tentacles coming together over the center of your being. Receive a blue-violet flame from your assistance. Use this flame to completely burn through any and all cords sent or received from a place of less than love. Allow them to be disintegrated and transmuted into light and love. Establish heart-to-heart connections with all by visualizing pure, white threads of light growing outward from your heart center and connecting with the white threads of light coming outwards from the heart center of others. Infuse this connection with the frequency of unconditional love.

Energy Fields

Your energy field consists of the seven layers of your auric field, forming a three dimensional oval around your physical being. Just as everything that you have ever thought, felt, experienced or witnessed is recorded in your DNA, resonances of these things are stored in your energetic field. High vibrational aspects are beneficial and assist you in coming into alignment with divine purpose and in the creation of a heart-centered reality. Low vibrational aspects or experiences you have perceived to be negative or harmful, act as obstacles and impede the path to heart-centered creation.

Experiences, thoughts and emotions that you have not been able to adequately process, release and learn from, gravitate closer and closer to your physical body until one day you wake up and you start to have pain that you can't correlate to a physical event. This is what is commonly referred to as pain with ambiguous onset. Over time, it becomes more and more noticeable until it affects your ability to complete activities of daily living. It fills your thoughts and compromises your emotional state. Perhaps it manifests in the form of low back pain, frozen shoulder syndrome or stiffness in your neck and shoulders. Maybe it takes another route and shows up as constipation, headaches or fibromyalgia. Whatever its form, it wants your attention. It is trying to tell you something, trying to encourage you to see things differently, from a higher perspective. Once you are willing to listen and to learn, the pain goes away. Interruptions to these signals may be introduced by medications or other forms of care that cover up the symptom, while the root cause remains unheard and is still lingering under the surface. However, these messages are persistent in attempts to be heard and they will find another form in which to manifest.

Your low back pain is dulled by muscle relaxers and steroid shots, but now you can't sleep at night. Your acid reflux is pacified by over-the-counter proton pump inhibitors, but now you have headaches. The cycle continues on until learning takes place. You finally forgive yourself and ease up on self-judgment. You accept yourself for who you are and release the need or desire to rewrite your past and, instead, embrace the present and plan for the future. Sometimes, this unfolds subconsciously and, one day, you wake up and you start to feel better. Sometimes, you may need a little help to see that which needs to be seen before feeling better is a possibility.

When backed by intention, you will experience great benefit from regular clearing of your energetic field. Through conscious completion of this exercise you are saying, **"I am willing, I allow and I release all that no longer serves. I choose to move forward in a new way, in accordance with the divine love that lives and grows within me in infinite abundance"**. This is a practical way to "clean out the cobwebs" from your field and ensures that you are receiving only the highest and most beneficial guidance, free from distortion. Consider adding this to your daily routine.

Energy Field Clearing: Place both hands on your heart. On an inhale breath, bring energy down from heaven and up from the center of the earth, merging the two in your heart chakra. Exhale this energy up from your heart and out through your crown chakra, allowing it to rain down into your energy field and purify your aura, releasing all interference to love. Inhale, breathing pure and unconditional love into your heart. Exhale, allowing love to diffuse outward until it completely fills every cell of your body. Repeat this cycle three to five times until you feel a lightening of your emotional load and receive the sense that you have released all that can be released in the moment.

Physical Pain

The source of physical aches and pains may be directly correlated to physical trauma, as in a sprained ankle or a burn after touching something hot. It is also possible that physical pain may be rooted in emotional trauma, as previously discussed. This could be the case in low back pain initiated by being laid off work or recently divorced, or as the result of feeling unsupported. Regardless of the source of physical pain, Creation energy may be used to ease it.

First, intuitively ask if the source of your pain is rooted in your physical body. If the answer is "yes", ask your body to reveal the exact location. Remember, you are asking for the source of the pain. This could mean that the pain you are experiencing in your knee is coming from structural dysfunction in your hip. By asking these questions you are able to direct energy to the root cause. If you are experiencing pain in your knee and your body reveals your knee to be the source of the pain, then direct the energy there. If the answer is "no", consider that the root cause of your physical discomfort may be coming from an energetic disturbance somewhere in your auric field. Intuitively look for the source of the disturbance and direct the energy there.

Be aware that your ego may try to convince you that the source of your pain is physical, even when it is not. This is especially relevant when pain is ambiguous in nature, coming on slowly, over time, and unrelated to any physical hurt or trauma. If you direct energy to a physical location and there is no change in the amount of pain you are experiencing, this indicates that you have probably not found the root cause. Ensure that you have removed all energetic blindfolds, earmuffs and earplugs, and open yourself to hear the truth from heart-centered space and start over. Each time this technique is completed, more and more pain will be released. Consider adding this to your daily energy routine until the pain is no longer present. To maximize your efforts, consider doing this in conjunction with additional modalities, such as chiropractic, physical therapy, massage, etc.

Easing Physical Pain: Discern the source or root cause of your pain. Begin concentrating Creation energy, formed in your heart where Source energy and Earth energy merge, at the root of your pain. Allow the energy to build, surrounding and perfusing your pain, filling it with unconditional love and healing. Remember, in working with Creation energy, you are pulling in a range of frequencies for healing and vibrational correction. This technique may be completed through intentional direction of the energy, or you may use your hands to direct the energy. Continue until the pain is reduced or until a sense of completion is experienced.

Note: You may be guided to energetically "pull" the pain out of your body or field. Pick it up with your hand and, using a counterclockwise motion, begin to pull it out. Fill the pain with light and send it into the earth to be transmuted into love.

The Twelve Rays of God

The Twelve Rays of God (also known simply as the Twelve Rays or the Twelve Healing Rays) are light beams of energy that offer creative and healing support. They are overseen by Archangels and Ascended Masters and are on the planet to clear away falsities and bring forth truth. They may be used in accordance with Activating Ascension for the transmutation of obstacles and in the creation of the forward path, through creation of a new energetic grid (Chapter 8). To learn more about the Twelve Rays, see the Suggested Reading list (Appendix D).

The Twelve Rays: Intuitively discern how many and which Rays would like to assist you in this clearing. They are named by their number. Allow them to come into your field and become aware of where they are centered. If you experience difficulty in discerning their presence, consider the agenda being cleared. Tune in to the location in your body, or energy field, in which this group of obstacles is being stored. Trust that this is the location in which the rays will be focused. Welcome in the presence of the overseers of these rays and thank them for their assistance. While comfortably positioned, close your eyes and visualize these rays around you, pouring their light inside. After a few moments of being filled with light, the tips of the rays will connect to form a ring of energy from which a new creation grid will be synergistically woven. When there is a recognizable shift in the intensity of the agenda, your work with the Twelve Rays is complete.

Erasing Mental Matrices

A mental matrix is the energetic grid, or womb, in which beliefs, understandings and perceptions of self and of how the world works are rooted and nourished. These matrices are like the speakers for the background noise playing in your mind. Some of them are beneficial and assist you as you walk through life: I am smart, funny, creative, etc. False matrices have the opposite effect and can be detrimental to successfully creating as you would like: I am dumb, not good enough, never going to succeed, etc. Erasing the mental matrix removes the energetic support for false beliefs that do not serve, allowing for transmutation of the false belief.

Erasing Mental Matrices is a clearing of the slate so that you may experience a new beginning. Without the matrix, the false belief is unable to attach, grow or fester within you. It is transmuted into love as the vibratory environment is too high for its existence.

In the usage of this technique within the context of Activating Ascension, you will know which matrix to erase, based upon the false belief listed under your obstacles on your Session Guide. For example, if you intuited that the false mental matrix of "everyone is out to get me" is acting as an obstacle standing in between you and manifestation of your intention, then this is the matrix with which to begin. This same technique is used to clear inherited belief obstacles.

When using this technique out of context of an Activating Ascension session, consider any false beliefs you may be holding and the associated mental matrix you would like to erase. Allow conscious awareness of those that no longer serve to rise from heart-centered space. Make a list and intuitively determine the highest priority. Understand that each time this technique is completed, more and more of the frequencies holding the false belief in place are deactivated until the matrix has been fully erased.

Erasing Mental Matrices: Visualize yourself surrounded by a pod of charged white light and allow the current to flow between your seven major chakras, linking them together and establishing pathways for higher dimensional communication. Consider using a personalized number activation sequence, color or shape to release any resistance that may arise.

To initiate frequency deactivation, you will be linking eye positions with hand positions, held on or a couple of inches above various locations on your body. These positions are intuitively determined and there may be more than one position to hold. Listen for clear guidance. Possible eye positions include: up, down, left, right, up and to the left, up and to the right, down and to the left, down and to the right. Hand positions could be anywhere on the body or hovering in your energy field. Once your hands and eyes are in place, meditate on the false belief and associated matrix you would like to release. Allow them to be transmuted into pure white light and unconditional love. Hold the positions until a shift is felt.

Complete the deactivation with the following breathing exercise: Stand, feet shoulder width apart and knees slightly bent. Inhale deeply, while bringing your palms together overhead in prayer position. While maintaining prayer position, exhale forcefully, quickly bringing your arms and hands down the center of your body to the floor. Repeat three to five times to ground the release.

Positive Imprinting

This technique replaces the false mental matrix released in the previous technique with a positive matrix, through frequency activation, to support you in new and beneficial ways. This imprint is placed directly into your DNA to assist in the facilitation of conscious evolution and transcension of the illusion. This is a reprogramming of your mental cues and the music you will now hear coming through the speakers of your mind will inspire the creation of a new reality. You will find yourself creating more successfully and with less difficulty after each repetition of this technique.

Begin by considering what you would like your new matrix to say. Anything is possible. Focus on transforming the sentiment of the previously released false mental matrix into something that you would like to emanate. The world is ready for you to step out boldly and is anticipating your decision to do so. This exercise will create a shift in self-perception that will radiate outward until all have been touched by it. This will create the space in others for positive self perception. With these imprints, you are laying the foundation for your new reality. Examples of matrices for positive imprinting include: I am love, I am peace, I am healed, I am whole.

Positive Imprinting: Once you have decided which matrix to imprint, begin to come into alignment with how life will look and feel when those statements are true. Saturate every cell with that sentiment, allowing its energy to access your genetic code. Use a personalized number activation sequence, color, shape or sound to assist you in releasing any resistance that may arise. Feel this fully before continuing.

Your personal will may be overshadowing your divine will. This will cause interference and inhibit the full benefits of the new mental matrix you have chosen. Bring them into alignment, before completing this technique. On an inhale breath, commit to the merging of personal and divine will, for your highest good. As you exhale, allow it to be done. Visualize yourself surrounded by an oval shaped, silver ring of light, vertically oriented so that it tapers above your head and below your feet. As you look at the left side of the ring you will notice that it may be tarnished, dented or even broken in some places. This half of the ring represents times in your life when personal will triumphed over divine will and the results led you further away from your divine purpose. As you look at the right side of the ring, you will notice it glimmering with love, truth and the promise of divine connection. This half of the ring represents the moments of your life when personal will surrendered to divine will and the results led you further along the path of divine purpose.

Allow the energy within the ring to begin circulating, simultaneously in both directions. Watch as any traces of tarnish or wear are transmuted and you are left with a brilliant ring of silver light, ready to divinely guide your way while honoring personal hopes and desires.

The process of encoding the physical body with positive imprinting begins once the ring is restored. Breathe deeply throughout, releasing all resistance. You may be able to physically feel the opening and clearing of energetic pathways within your body. This will subside as the flow of energy is restored.

Focus your breath on bringing fresh oxygen directly into the nucleus of each cell, providing a nutrient rich environment for completion of this update to your genetic code. With every breath the signal gets amplified and the positive imprint is replicated layer upon layer until it feels like it was a part of your being from the very beginning. Once the positive imprint begins to resonate as truth, initiation of the upgrade is complete.

Impulses

Impulses offer quantum leaps in consciousness during moments when divine timing coincides with a strong desire for heart expansion. For example, one such moment may occur prior to getting married when there is a strong desire to release fear of inadequacy and grow, in love, with a partner for life. Or, prior to college graduation when there is a strong desire to be open-hearted enough to receive the abundance the universe has to offer. Not all such moments will be as consciously significant as these examples, though they will be just as relevant. The offering, reception and activation of impulses has been happening your entire life. They have been unconsciously accepted to encourage expansion, or denied because of unwillingness on the part of the ego to relinquish control.

Impulses expand the bandwidth of frequencies to which you have access to for the purpose of creation. Through a heightened sense of awareness, and in the context of an Activating Ascension session, you will now have opportunity to consciously receive, accept and activate impulses.

Impulse Activation: Awareness of the opportunity to accept and receive an offered impulse will arise intuitively as you are guided to this technique, either while in prayerful meditation or in the completion of a healing or clearing session. Open yourself to receive the reason for its offering and allow it to rise from heart centered space. Once you understand why it's being offered, decide if you are ready to receive it. When you have consciously given your permission, receive the impulse into your heart and allow it to be activated. The impulse will come in the form of a

124

personalized symbol, specifically for you. It is slightly more beneficial if you have some awareness of the symbol, though it is not necessary. Once in your heart, allow the activation to radiate outwards to your entire being for genetic integration. It is complete when consciousness registers the symbol as intrinsically part of you.

Remember, as your vibration rises and higher frequencies within your grid are activated, anything causing dissonance will have to leave. Be prepared for feelings of anger, fear or irritation to rise to the surface to be released. Breathe deeply and allow them to go. Use a personalized number activation sequence, color, shape or sound to release resistance to their leaving. Compliant follow up will mitigate these reactions.

Wholeness

The sum of the whole is greater than its parts. To efficiently and effectively create from the heart, it is recommended that you transition closer and closer towards wholeness, claiming the essence of self, while releasing all that does not belong. Life experiences sometimes result in an energetic exchange of soul pieces. This is a progression of sending and receiving cords, during times of high emotion, when intentions have been less than heart centered. This happens subconsciously when facing loss, grief, guilt or when consumed with hate, bitterness or the need for revenge. What began with a cord, could end in this exchange. It may be challenging to move forward when pieces of yourself are missing or when carrying extra ones that do not belong.

The following exercise brings back your missing pieces and returns pieces that are not yours, to their rightful owners. It also allows for healing of any wounded aspects of your soul self, helping you to detach from your story. In order for the exchange to complete, open your heart with willingness and acceptance to send and receive them. You will be able to send pieces that are ready for release. You will be able to receive pieces that you are ready to assimilate and integrate into the whole. Each time this technique is completed, you will come closer and closer to wholeness.

Creating Wholeness: Begin by surrounding yourself in a three dimensional heart, filled with emerald green light. Send out eight threads of white light from the center of your heart, in all directions. Anchor them into the heart that encompasses you, with white stars. Claim a space of unconditional love. Breathe this love in, filling your lungs, heart and blood vessels with its energy. Allow love to perfuse your entire being and begin bringing all pieces that are ready to be returned to others to the surface.

As these pieces rise, call them together, over your heart center. Visualize any energetic cords or threads holding these pieces bound and use the blue-violet flame, from your assistance, to burn through them, allowing them to be disintegrated into light and love. Set your intention to release these pieces, returning them to their rightful owners, filled with unconditional love and gratitude for all they have taught you. Trust that they will be healed and made whole and integrated where they belong, with ease and grace, in the now moment. Allow the return of all such pieces before continuing. Fill all the spaces left behind with unconditional love and gratitude. Raise the vibration of those spaces so high, that nothing less than love could ever thrive there again.

Turn your attention to the missing pieces of your soul that you would now like to retrieve. Begin by creating space for them within your being, on a cellular level, by visualizing two white stars, rotating in opposite directions, spiraling through your being. Use a cosmic vacuum to clear away impurities blocking the return path.

Send out a beacon of light from your heart chakra to begin calling all missing pieces back to you, healed and made whole. If they are attached into the fields of others by cords or threads, offer the blue-violet flame to assist in their release. Allow all returning pieces to be integrated into your being with ease and grace in the now moment, on a cellular level, for your highest good. Visualize those from whom your pieces have been returned, being filled with unconditional love and gratitude. Allow integration to complete before continuing.

Offer any aspects of your soul self, that are wounded or bind you to fear, up for healing. Release these pieces to the Divine Creator, trusting that they will be healed and made whole, transmuted in light and love. Receive the blue-violet flame to disintegrate any cords or threads holding them bound. The pieces that will assist you on your forward path will be returned over time. The pieces that no longer serve will be forever in the Creator's care. With the release of attachment to your story, comes grace. Fill any void or space left behind from this release with unconditional love and gratitude. Raise the vibration of these spaces so high, that nothing less than love could ever thrive there again. Allow this offering to complete before continuing.

Contracts

As was previously discussed in Chapter 4, contracts are binding agreements to bring about life circumstances that help you learn lessons, predetermined by you and your Spiritual Support Team, prior to incarnation, for the benefit of your conscious evolution. As old contracts expire, or fail due to free will choices, new ones are organized by your higher self while in physical body. Their purpose is to guide you through lessons that may seem undesirable on the surface, though are beneficial for your spiritual growth and heart-centered expansion. The human experience unfolds through transitions in adversity. For love, kindness, compassion and unity to resonate as divine truths, one must typically experience their illusory lack.

Examples of contracts include: poverty, silence, celibacy, servitude, obedience, being less than, resisting divinity, denying mastery, illness, relationships, sabotage, inter-dimensional agreements and more. Successful navigation of these leads to a profound understanding of the human experience and what it means to transcend the physical world. The lessons they have to offer may be realized in a singular lifetime, or their learning may span multiple incarnations. Once a contract has been completed, or reconfigured, all resonances of it are to be released.

When this does not happen, resonances of or emotional attachment to a completed contract may interfere with your ability to create, acting as an obstacle to your forward path. In such situations, conscious release of them is beneficial. Understand that all contracts have positive effects, even if not immediately recognizable. When successfully navigated, without resistance, they encourage the ability to live from love, without constraint or dependence on a material world.

Contract Dissolution: To release all resonances and emotional attachment to an identified and completed contract, begin by placing yourself in the center of a yellow sphere of light. Complete a personalized number activation sequence and use additional colors and shapes, or sound, to free any resistance to releasing the contract. Imagine the contract held in a book and visualize a black cord of light holding you bound together. Accept the blue-violet flame from your assistance and completely disintegrate the cord. Allow your assistance to carry the contract off to higher realms for complete transmutation into light and love. Celebrate its release with joyful movement.

Intuitive Understanding

The previously discussed intuition upgrade exercises are designed to clear intuitive channels and pathways so that guidance may be heard or otherwise perceived. The purpose of this technique is to bring you into alignment with your higher self and to assist you in clear understanding of the guidance coming forth, through movement. It will allow for expansion of what has previously been received and will help to fill in any missing pieces. Within the context of an Activating Ascension session, you will be guided to this technique when unable to clearly see how a particular obstacle applies as a block to intention.

Intuition Increase: Begin by stating an intention to align with Source so that guidance may rise from heart-centered space to conscious awareness with greater clarity and with ease and grace. Visualize your entire being filled with purple and orange light, radiating outwards, in all directions from your center. Stand, feet shoulder width apart, arms down by your sides.

Step 1: On an inhale breath bring your arms overhead.

Step 2: Exhale, turn towards the left and slowly make a large, vertically oriented infinity symbol with your arms.

Step 3: Inhale, return arms overhead.

Step 4: Exhale, brush your hands down over your face, heart and center line until they   rest on your feet, or hang freely. Take three deep breaths.

Step 5: Come up on an inhale breath while raising both arms over head, hands together in prayer position.

Step 6: As you exhale, lower your hands to rest at your heart. Repeat with a horizontally oriented infinity symbol overhead and then another vertically oriented one to your right. Repeat the entire process three times. Listen for the new insights that will come forth.

Note: Modifications may be made to this sequence as directed by physical ability. If you are unable to bend forward and touch your toes while standing, complete the sequence from a seated position. If this is not possible, breathe deeply and visualize its completion.

Programming Discs

Programming discs are small, energetic, colored disks for the purpose of removing faulty or outdated programming from your system and replacing it with updated versions that are in alignment with what you would like to create. Think of these as the body's antiviral software for the release of low vibrational thought forms, patterns and matrices and the activation of higher vibrational ones. One or several discs may be offered at a time. You will be able to correlate their specific function based on the agenda you are clearing and the intention you are manifesting. They will be offered to you from your assistance and come directly from Source.

To Accept Programming Discs: Begin with a personalized number activation sequence and use color, shape or sound to release resistance to shifts in consciousness. Visualize yourself in the center of a cube, interwoven with quartz crystal and opal. As the discs are offered, allow them to come into your being through your crown chakra, for automatic distribution to where they are required. As you visualize, feel or imagine their presence, you will know when you have received all that is being offered. Once they have been downloaded, allow reprogramming to fully complete before continuing.

Resentment

Resentment is born out of the ego's need to keep score, place blame and hold others accountable for your perception of unfairness. Resentments are bitter reactions to circumstances that, ultimately, you have contributed more to than you may be willing to realize. It is challenging, if not impossible, to create a heart-filled existence in any area of your life while harboring resentment in other areas. For example, holding resentment towards your mother for not giving you all you thought you needed, will permeate and shadow every other relationship whether or not you are consciously aware of its effects.

The first step to releasing resentments is to acknowledge them. Consider the specifics of those that contribute to the agenda you are clearing. Then, explore those that are contributing indirectly and begin releasing them too. Some of these resentments have been with you a long time and have hugely influenced who you are today and how you view the world. As your vibration rises, there is little space to carry them forward. Begin releasing them now with the following movement sequence. Release as much as you can in the moment and repeat when you are ready to release more. Allow resentments to fade away into nothingness, where they may no longer influence your ability to create.

Releasing Resentment: If balance is a challenge, keep your eyes open. If you find that too easy, close your eyes. Allow your spirit to be filled with the energy of aquamarine to instill courage for releasing the victim mentality. If you have an aquamarine stone, or two, hold them in your pockets throughout the exercise. As resistance rises to the surface, use numbers, color or shape for its release. Begin when you are ready, clearing one resentment at a time.

1. Stand with feet shoulder width apart, arms out by your sides, palms facing up, and say **"I willingly open and release (list your resentment here)."**

2. Stand on one foot and bring your arms overhead, palms together in prayer position and say: **"I understand that it is weakening the foundation upon which I am trying to create."**

3. Return to the starting position and say: **"I choose to release it and create upon a strong foundation."**

Repeat until the resentment is no longer weakening your foundation and you are able to stand on one foot with improved balance. By coupling the intention to release with physical movement, you are erasing the mental patterning that held your resentment in place.

Addictions

Addictions are points of fixation for the ego. Whenever the outside world fails to measure up to inner expectations, addictions provide the perfect distraction. They help fill the void of loneliness, isolation and insecurity. The energetic requirement to maintain addiction is high and this is why they leave you feeling exhausted and drained, once the initial gratification dissipates. Once the pattern for addiction is in place, it will consume your thoughts and your actions as you plot your next "fix". The obvious addictions are drugs, cigarettes and alcohol. Those that are less obvious, or less talked about, are addictions to sex, lying, food and disfigurement. Those hoping to escape scrutiny, include addictions to exhibitionism, failure, the need to be right, control and constant stimulation. The list goes on. What is it that you are addicted to? Used within the context of an Activating Ascension session, "addict" will reveal itself as a consciousness pattern, acting as an obstacle. Allow conscious awareness of the specific addiction to rise before continuing. Consider exploring this technique independent of Activating Ascension to free energy currently being consumed by addictions.

It is tempting to rationalize that your particular addiction is somehow less severe than someone else's. It is important to understand that, regardless of how an addiction is outwardly expressed, the cause is always the same. They are all egoic attempts to pacify the need to be loved, heard, seen, understood, and part of.

If you have been clinically diagnosed with addictive behaviors or participate in a twelve step program, understand that this technique is not a substitute for prescribed medical care. Use this technique in conjunction with the systems already in place. Repeat it daily for two weeks. Be consistent and compliant for the most beneficial results, even if you feel as though you are no longer affected by the addiction. A free will choice and willingness to quit are the energies that back this technique.

Freedom from Addictions: Begin by listening for a personalized number activation sequence. Use color, shape or sound to transmute any resistance to releasing addiction. Visualize yourself in the center of a fully-opened crystal rose. Fill your heart with red light, your throat with blue light and your head with pink light. Breathe deeply and infuse your being with compassion.

Allow conscious awareness of the very first time you did that which you desire to stop, to rise from heart-centered space. Watch as all relevant images, thoughts and words materialize, trusting that you are seeing exactly what you need to see. Imagine a portal opening up that will transport you back in time to the moment right before you first _____ (fill in the blank: overate, smoked, lied, drank alcohol, etc.). Establish a heart-to-heart connection with that version of yourself, as white light pours through you into your prior self. As both of you are filled with the light of Divine love, ask this former version of yourself what he/she needs to feel whole. Unconditional love, acceptance, approval, compassion and connection are all possibilities. Fill them with all that is needed until the desire, for that which you long to quit, dissipates. Once all that may be given has been received, come back through the portal and return to the present moment.

Love Infusions

The power of love has the ability to shift consciousness away from poverty, war and hatred to compassion, understanding and peace. Bringing love to light in all situations is the catalyst for illuminating the darkness. Wherever you are, when you radiate love, you have a profound effect on a global scale. Love Infusions cast away all doubt within the one radiating love, the one receiving love and all of mass consciousness, as to the true nature and prime purpose of the human experience: the expression of love in all thoughts, words and actions. Use this technique within the context of an Activating Ascension session to prime the release of obstacles eliciting strong emotional resistance. Use it in your everyday life because it feels good. Begin with relationships and situations close to you and then turn toward causes greater than your own.

Infusing with Love: It is difficult to love others unconditionally before unconditionally loving yourself. Begin with a personalized number activation sequence and use color, shape or sound to release any resistance to accepting love into your heart. Visualize the stream of brilliant white light that connects your heart into the heart of Source. If you cannot see it, imagine it. If it is dimmed, or otherwise diminished, allow it to be cleansed and purified, harmonized and amplified for your greatest good. Begin to feel the infinite abundance of unconditional love flowing into you from the heart of a Divine Creator. Bask in this love before continuing.

Imagine that your heart is a channel for pure and unconditional love. As your heart is open, love continually fills and flows through it. Love sees all of your flaws and imperfections and knows that you are a beautiful and wonderful child of the universe, worthy of all that love has to give. Begin to focus your attention on an obstacle, situation, relationship, friend or stranger in need of healing love. Become aware of deficiencies of love. Concentrate love into darkness within this connection, bringing light to what has been hidden so that anything less than love may be transformed. Allow love to flow out of your heart, in a steady stream to another, until the heart of any resistance is awakened to light and remembers that love is the answer. Stay connected in this way until a sense of completion is felt. For the highest transformation, revisit this meditation four times for each relationship or situation.

Calibration of Global Positioning System

Just as the GPS in your car or on your phone will always lead you home, there is a similar system in place that keeps you connected with Source. When you move away from the location of your inception, in accordance with your divine path, your global positioning mechanism will be automatically calibrated to Source, from your new location. This, however, does not always happen if there is great resistance to your move or if the move has taken you off path and away from your divine purpose. It may make it difficult to feel a personal connection with a Divine Creator and you may be unable to feel at home in your new surroundings. If you are not feeling as though you belong, are homesick, or have trepidation about the reasons for your move or the region in which you are living, calibration of your global positioning system may be consciously accomplished with this technique. It may need to be repeated more than once, depending on the level of resistance held, or how far off path you have veered. This connection may also need calibrating if you are resisting a move that is in accordance with your divine path and purpose. Staying too long in a geographical location or environment that does not support you will have the same effects. Calibration, in this circumstance, may never fully complete.

Calibration: To calibrate your connection with Source, begin by listening for a personalized number activation sequence. Surround yourself in a crystal blue diamond and visualize threads of silver and golden light moving up and down your spine. With your eyes closed, energetically connect with the place of your inception. Your heart may reveal images, words or other details to assist in the connection. Otherwise, allow the feeling of "home" to fill your being. Upon this feeling, ask your assistance to reset coordinates for your global positioning mechanism for reconnection with Source. This connection will be encoded into the silver and golden threads of light in your spine, strengthening your personal relationship with a Divine Creator.

Surrendering Ego

Fulfillment of the Activating Ascension purpose rests in the ability to surrender ego. This creates the space for the opening, emergence and expansion of the heart that will lead the entire world into the creation of a heart-centered reality. Attuning to the new creation grid, through which this energetic construct will be manifested, assists in the release of cords holding one back to the old creation grid. (You will learn more about the creation grid and have opportunity to complete the attunement in Part III). However, for the transition from the old to the new to complete, the old grid (upon which the ego thrives) is to be completely dissolved. This transition has already been initiated and is happening slowly, in accordance with the increasing vibration of mass consciousness. In using this technique to release obstacles to your intention, you are adding efficiency to this transition.

Though you may not completely understand the implications, many of you reading these words are keepers of the grid. If this is the case for you, more information and guidance will be revealed over time. Until then, know that your participation in this transition is helping to clear for the collective consciousness for release of the old paradigm of separation, lack and fear.

Dissolution of the Grid: Begin by surrounding yourself in a merkaba (a three-dimensional star of David), filled with radiant white light. Listen for a personalized number activation sequence and use color, shape or sound to release any resistance you may be holding. Honor the old creation grid, filling it with love and gratitude for all it has shown and taught you. Visualize it being filled with the same radiant white light as your merkaba. Become consciously aware of the cords holding you bound to the old grid. Cut the ones to which you have access and begin anchoring them into the new grid. Allow your cords to be received by the awaiting guide posts of the new grid. Hold the intention for a smooth transition from the old grid to the new one. Celebrate and amplify this new energetic connection and embrace the energy of love, unity and abundance. Radiate it out to the world.

Kristyn

This is an example of unexpected benefits from energetic clearing and balancing. I had been working with Kristyn for a couple of months on the intentions of confidence in decision making and the mastery of time management. At the end of one of our phone sessions, this conversation unfolded:

Kristyn: *"I've always been allergic to dogs, but when I was around one last weekend, I didn't have any reaction. Could what we've been doing have caused that?"*

Me: *"Absolutely! Environmental allergies come from issues in the gut. Much of our work has been focused on healing your digestive system through rewiring of the energetic balance within your solar plexus."*

Additionally, Kristyn has become more assertive in asking for what she needs and has come to the understanding that her high-stress career is no longer serving her highest good. She is actively seeking different employment and is confident in her decision to do so.

Chapter 7: Closing an Activating Ascension Session

You've learned how to open a session, identify the corresponding agendas and obstacles and the techniques to clear them. All that remains is to close your session. The purpose of the opening sequence is to come into heart centered space, release ego and define your intention while opening yourself to receive assistance through divine guidance. In closing, the focus is shifted from preparation to integration of the healing that has taken place and intuiting the steps that will assist you in moving forward. This involves filling the void, requesting integration, determining processing time, following up to mitigate or amplify reactions to release, developing an action plan and offering up the healing you've received to anyone who would like to claim it as their own. It only takes a few moments to complete and will allow a deeper understanding of what to expect and how to move forward. These steps bring clarification of the bigger picture. To receive the greatest benefit from your session, complete each step.

Fill the Void

Everything, including thoughts, emotions and experiences, has energy and takes up space. Filling the void ensures that the vibration of the space left behind, as a result of release, is raised so high that nothing less than love can ever thrive within it. Whenever an agenda, or group of obstacles, has been released, fill that space with love and gratitude so that there is no room or need for them to ever be manifested again. This step is your insurance against recreating undesirable circumstances and experiences.

Fill the space with unconditional love for yourself first and then for everyone else. This unconditional love represents your ability to recognize your inner divinity, as well as the divinity in others. This love creates the space and holds the container for a shift in perspective that allows gratitude to permeate your life experiences. When the ego is surrendered, everything that has happened, is happening or will happen may be viewed through conscious detachment as opportunities for growth, learning and spiritual evolution. This perspective allows no room for blame and no reason to withhold forgiveness from yourself or others.

Fill the Void: Close your eyes, breathe deeply and visualize all empty spaces being filled with love and gratitude. You may do this through intention, or you may ask your assistance for a personalized symbol that represents love and gratitude to you. Visualize this symbol permeating the void. Send it out in all directions from your heart center. Understand that anyone involved with perceived negative experiences has helped you learn valuable lessons. In accepting the lessons, and in learning them, you are able to release them completely and permanently. There is no need to recreate them again.

Request Integration

Requesting integration voices your energetic commitment to creating your life based upon a newfound perspective, in alignment with your highest good and free from attachment. Integration internalizes these concepts so that the highest vibrational response possible is automatically given in any situation. Over time, your karmic debt will be cleared and your vibration will be of such that no new karma will be generated.

Energetic releases or clearings rearrange your neuronal circuitry, breaking connections that no longer serve and forming new connections of a higher vibration. For full integration to take place, a reboot of your physical, mental, emotional and spiritual systems is recommended. Just as you would reboot your computer after an update, requesting integration optimizes your ability to hold a higher vibration.

You may choose to complete this through intention or prayer. When integrating with intention, visualize your heart being filled with white light. Allow the light to radiate outwards to your entire being, cleansing and purifying all thoughts, emotions and other toxins that no longer serve your highest and best good. Visualize golden light spiraling up and down and all around your body to seal in the healing power of the white light.

If your preference is to integrate through prayer, consider this example: "Mother, Father, God, Creator of all that is, please assist me in fully integrating this new level of healing on a cellular level with ease and grace in the now moment. Synchronize my vibration with the vibration of the greater good. Bring me into alignment with my divine purpose that I may positively impact my life, my family and my world. Raise my awareness and assist me in the transmutation of all things less than love. So be it and so it is."

141

Processing Time

Processing time represents the amount of time required for full and complete integration. What happens in the moment of working with this system is only the beginning. The transformation will continue to unfold over a span of time. It may be hours, days, months or years. To allow for the highest levels of ease and grace, do not begin another Activating Ascension session for the intention you have set, prior to completion of the processing time. Understand that this is a caution against clearing too much too quickly in ways that will not be easily integrated. Vibration rises through a shift of frequencies in a range. Vibrations beyond the top of the range are activated as vibrations at the bottom end of the range are simultaneously deactivated. Drastic shifts in range are uncomfortable and make it difficult to interact with the physical world. Smaller shifts are more easily integrated, allowing for a smoother transition to higher vibrations.

Ask your higher self and your assistance how long to allow for complete processing of your session. Make a note of this on your Session Guide (Appendix C). If there are additional clearings to be completed, return to the session upon completion of the processing time. If all agendas to the original intention have been cleared, consider you next intention and begin again.

Follow Up

Completion of follow up maximizes ease of processing and integration. Commit to its completion after each session. Typically, follow up steps are simple and easily worked into your daily routine. Be consistent. Your follow up will amplify positive reactions to release and mitigate any negative reactions that may arise.

For ideas, consult the "Follow Up" column of Part I of the Activating Ascension Tools Table (Appendix B). You will rarely have more than three steps to complete after any given session. Listen for as many details regarding each step as possible. For example, intuitively ask: how much, how often, when, for how long, etc. Possibilities include, but are not limited to: being in nature, meditating, movement, devoting time for yourself, doing something creative, hydration, nutrition and sound/toning/music.

Note: If you are intuitively called to the "Supplement/Homeopathic" column as part of your follow up, consider the list as a foundational starting point. It is not comprehensive. If you have a nutritional background or strong understanding of nutritional basics, trust your intuition and ask that the most beneficial supplements be revealed to you. If you have any questions or hesitation, seek professional advice from a holistic nutritionist, an herbalist or homeopathic physician.

Reactions to Release

After an Activating Ascension clearing, you will start to notice changes in your life. Some of these will be subtle and happen over time, others will be more noticeable. Some will happen effortlessly and others may seem difficult at the time. Completing your follow up exercises will mitigate negative reactions and amplify positive ones.

Ease and grace are built into this system. As obstacles are removed, deeper and more hidden issues come rising to the surface. It may not always appear that they do so with ease and grace, but consider what it might look like if that were not the built-in intention. The key to releasing that which no longer serves is to flow through the process without resistance. If ever you experience difficulty, consider where you are holding resistance and focus on releasing it. You will learn additional techniques for releasing resistance in Part III.

Consult the "Reactions to Release" column of Part I of the Activating Ascension Tools Table (Appendix B), for a better understanding of possible reactions. Intuitively ask how many and then identify each. Having an understanding of the possibility of reactions will make them easier to mitigate if they arise.

Action Plan

Up to this point, the focus has been on clearing agendas that have prevented your intention from being manifested into reality. Your Action Plan is formulated as your path is cleared. This involves identification of all of the steps to be taken in order to manifest your intention, or reach your goal. The first question you may consider asking is: **"What can I do today to realize my intention?"** The answer you receive may include all necessary steps or the steps that must be taken before more clearing is required. A few steps will be revealed at a time so that you will not be overwhelmed. Complete these first and then ask what is next. For example, if you have been working on weight loss, your first steps may include reading a particular book on holistic nutrition and reducing the amount of sugar that you are consuming. Or, you may be directed to consult a nutritionist to get you started. Consult the "Action Plan" column of Part I of the Activating Ascension Tools Table (Appendix B), for more ideas to get you started.

Action planning will come easiest when you have been able to release resistance to moving forward and attachment to the outcome and the steps that you "think" will lead you there. Whenever you hear yourself saying "I think that this would be the best course of action", stop. This is an indication that you have come out of heart-centered space and into the realm of mind and ego. Go with what "feels" right. Your heart knows exactly what to do. If you have released resistance and attachment and are still experiencing difficulty with the step, consider asking for outside assistance from a close and trusted friend, a life coach or a spiritual guide.

Share Your Release

The world is in need of healing on many levels. Chances are that millions of others are experiencing hardships similar to what you will be clearing through use of this system. Share your release with them. After each session, offer it to anyone with the desire to claim it for themselves. Know that while you cannot override free will and force anyone to receive a healing when it is not their choice, you can place the healing in their energy field for them to either choose to accept or not. Simply say: **"I now offer up this new level of healing to anyone who would like to accept it, with ease and grace and for the greater good of all humanity in the now moment."** Sharing your release answers a call to service and represents a higher contribution to the evolution of mass consciousness. People all over the world will benefit from what you've offered even though they have no conscious awareness of it. The vibration of humanity as a whole will rise. Understand that as you are offering up your experience of healing, others will be doing the same for you. Be aware and open to receive these into your heart as they arise in your field.

Closing the Sacred Circle

Your session is now complete. Close your sacred circle and express gratitude for all of the assistance that came to help. Know that you will have their continued love and support. Closing your sacred circle is a means of showing your appreciation,

145

disconnecting from your session and grounding once again into physical reality.

Example: "To all the beings and energies of high light and vibration that participated in this sacred circle, I humbly express my sincere gratitude for all of your help. Please continue to impart your wisdom, knowledge and love. Use me as a channel for your healing works in this world. With love and gratitude in my heart, I close the sacred circle."
Recap of the closing sequence: Fill the void, request integration and determine length of processing time. Intuit follow up recommendations and possible reactions. Make a note of action steps to be taken. Offer up your healing to the world and close your sacred circle.

You now have everything you need to complete an Activating Ascension session. To see how it all comes together, the entire process is explained in Appendix A, the Activating Ascension Step-By-Step guide and is visually presented in Appendix C, the Session Guide. The Tools Tables are included in Appendix B. Familiarize yourself with these and begin your first session. Remember, energy follows intention. There is no requirement for perfection in order to attain the desired results. Anytime you learn something new, there is an associated learning curve. The more the process is repeated, the easier it becomes. To gain efficiency or a deeper understanding than the written word provides, or to become an Activating Ascension Practitioner, consider attending an Activating Ascension retreat (www.activatingascension.com).

Closing a Session: Recap

Fill the Void
Request Integration
Determine Processing time
Follow Up
Reactions to Release
Action Plan
Share Your Release
Close Sacred Circle

Part III: Creating Consciously

Chapter 8: Grids and Attunement

Grids

A grid is the energetic matrix or framework for creation. All of life and all thoughts and ideas begin with a grid - from a single cell, to a plant, animal or human, from the core of the Earth, to the land and water that covers it, from the cure for smallpox, to the building of the internet. Everything is made according to its grid and each grid is made according to its divine blueprint. In other words, all is made according to the divine instruction that inspired its manifestation. As the grid is able to vibrate in accordance with its divine blueprint, the highest expression results. This is the natural state of the universe, observable when the planet and all life upon it coexist symbiotically in harmonious and sustainable ways.

Creation grids fall out of alignment when they are unable to resonate with their divine blueprint and their highest expression is no longer possible. In humans, this lowering of vibration occurs when the ego introduces artifacts into the grid that negatively impact the grid's capacity to hold the space for creation. Artifacts are constructs of the ego formed out of competition, greed, sorrow, lack, separation and fear.

Grids are made of frequencies that direct and layer patterns of light until an idea that was once intangible is manifested into physical form. There are an infinite number of grids in existence. Some work independently while others intersect or overlap to create new grids or affect different outcomes. Grids may be localized, inter-dimensional, or intergalactic. Some transcend constructs of time and space. Access to creation grids, and their frequencies, is governed by the vibration of the individual or group trying to access them. The more aligned with Source, the greater the access to higher frequencies and the grids formed by them.

This is an extremely complicated and intricately interwoven concept. In efforts to keep the following explanation accessible, focus will be placed upon the intersection point of all grids coming into Earth's field and the crystalline grid emanating outward from the Earth's center. This intersection takes place in your heart and forms your creation grid, the matrix in which your life manifested.

Creation Grids

Your creation grid represents the sum total number of frequencies to which you have access and is filled with creation energy to assist you in evolution and growth. Creation grids vary significantly from person to person, based upon the vibration of each. As one comes into higher alignment, their creation grid will shift to accommodate higher frequencies and allow for the deactivation of lower frequencies. Conversely, should one fall out of alignment, their grid will shift accordingly.

The mass consciousness creation grid is undergoing a restructuring to assist in the evolution of conscious awareness. Time capsules within the Earth's crust are being activated to allow for the assimilation of frequencies that have remained dormant since the last age of enlightenment. Solar flares are the primary source of frequencies coming into the Earth.

These energetic shifts in frequency are resulting in the rewiring of consciousness on a grand scale. For some, these shifts have been anticipated and are being effortlessly integrated. For those harboring resistance to change, this process has been more challenging. Eventually, the current grid for conscious creation will be completely replaced by a new one. This transition will evolve slowly to allow for maximal levels of ease and grace. See the following table for characteristics and governing principles of each.

Current Creation Grid	New Creation Grid
Governed by the ego	Governed by the Heart
Duality	Oneness
Change is hard	Change is beneficial
You have to do it all by yourself	Cooperation
Isolation	Unity
Separation	Community
Force	Power
Lack	Abundance
Fear	Love
Worry	Trust
Limited	Unlimited

You may choose to consciously assist in the release of the old grid and in the transition into the new one. The energetics of this shift are already in motion. It will not be stopped or reversed, though its speed is influenced by the willingness of mass consciousness to evolve. Holding resistance to these changes and remaining rooted and anchored in the old grid will prove challenging as the transition progresses. Consciously connecting to the new grid will allow for much more ease and grace, affording a supportive energetic environment from which to create.

There are several ways to begin releasing the old grid and connecting to the new one. Each time they are completed, additional attachments will be transitioned from the old to the new. Consistent efforts to surrender ego and live from the heart, through Activating Ascension or other means, will help initiate, foster and nurture transition. Participating in the following attunement is another way. Or, you may release the energetic cords or threads holding you anchored in the old grid and allow new ones to generate for anchoring into the new grid through intention. These examples are not comprehensive. There are thousands of ways to consciously promote this shift.

There is an abundance of information being shared about the specifics of these changes, through many different channels. Some of the information is contradictory and/or confusing. It is not that certain channels are "right" while others are "wrong", it is simply a matter of to whom the information is applicable. Everyone is on an individual path to ascension, therefore some information will apply to you, where you are. And, if it doesn't resonate as truth to you, it likely applies to others who are in a different place on their journey. Use discernment and focus on what feels right to you.

Jessica

My patients leave the Initial Visit with the understanding that they did not create their current circumstances overnight and that it will likely take time and effort to create something different. I think that sometimes we, as alternative healers, place unrealistic expectations upon ourselves. We read the success stories of others and assume that spectacular results are achieved in one session. When this doesn't happen, the ego is quick to condemn. Through personal experiences with this idea, I learned to set realistic goals and timelines with patients so that they know up front that what I'm offering is not a quick fix. I also learned to celebrate the subtle successes that sometimes go unnoticed.

When Jessica came in for her third visit, her energy was different. I asked her how she was feeling and she responded, "I don't know how to put it into words, but I'm a different person now. I feel stronger, like I can do anything - including creating financial prosperity! When I went into work yesterday, a colleague asked me what I've been doing. She said that everything about me looked totally different. I just smiled and told her that I AM different."

Optional Attunement

This attunement will create an initiation pathway for evolution of consciousness in alignment with the heart grid. An audio recording of it is available at www.activatingascension.com. It will help you release cords to the ego grid for anchoring into the heart, in a way that is easily integrated into your being, in the now moment, with grace. It will minimize resistance, while cultivating open-heartedness and the ability to create from love. Begin the attunement with the Activating Ascension opening sequence, and finish with the closing sequence. This attunement is overseen by Kali, Jesus, Buddha, Isis, Gaia, Amaterasu, Abraham and Krishna. You will hear several number activation sequences to assist in the activation and deactivation of frequencies within your grid. Set your intention to receive all additional numbers, specifically for you. To amplify the frequency shift offered by the attunement, complete it three times within two weeks and then once per month, until it is no longer in your highest and best to receive it.

Kali will initiate your attunement. She is the Hindu Goddess of time and change and is here to assist in the alchemical transmutation of egoic control. Jesus represents the embodiment of the Christ consciousness. His presence is to inspire unconditional love and forgiveness. Buddha, an enlightened being, teaches the value of detachment. He comes forth to interweave wisdom into love. Isis is the Divine Mother, cultivator of spiritual maturity and restoration of the divine feminine. Her presence is to awaken the depths of compassion from within. Gaia is the Earth, personified. She is here to assist in the birth of higher level consciousness and to awaken light codes within your DNA. Amaterasu is the Shinto Goddess of the sun and universe. Her presence serves to nullify polarity of thought and perception. Abraham offers the ability to overcome. He is a symbol of unwavering faith through universal surrender. Krishna is an avatar in the Hindu tradition and the ascended master that has pledged to assist in the healing of the inner child. He offers a return to innocence.

Attunement to the Heart

Close your eyes and sit comfortably, bare feet on the floor, palms facing upward in your lap. Connect the thumb and ring finger of your left hand, to form a ring. Hold the fingers of your right hand as though they were uncurling from a tightened ball. Allow the energy of your intention to be purified, balanced and amplified for your highest good. Breathe deeply and submerge into silence. Surround yourself in blue. Align with the void and empty your vessel into the abyss. Instruct your cellular filaments to relax and open. **39 8247 69197917917 4 23 8**. Sink deeper and deeper into heart-centered space until it feels as though you are weightless, freed from the constraints of physical form. **272727 298197917917 24824 92197**. Allow the script for your genetic expression to be recoded. **621947 9147 9147 9147**. Allow your consciousness to merge into oneness with the unified field. **24824 248 7 791847917**. Allow cellular memory to be accessed by the overseers of this attunement. **26 26 26 792419719427**.

Call forth your ego. Allow it to materialize in energetic form in the space in front of your heart, about two feet away. Become aware of the colored film in which it is encapsulated. If it is black or grey, visualize it being filled with white light. If it is brown, visualize it being filled with red light. If it is a combination of these colors, visualize your ego filled with golden light. If it is any other color, allow it to be filled with soft, purple light. Observe as the film is completely perfused by the light and begins to transform. Your ego is becoming lighter and its desire for control is softening. Create a braid of gold and silver light, growing it outward from the center of your heart and anchoring into the center of your ego with four doves of peace. Infuse this connection with love and gratitude for all your ego has done for you and fill it with the knowingness that it is safe to surrender. Allow it to be reintegrated into your being. **2391827918279 4 624823 7919 8 9189189**.

The sacred heart of the Christ consciousness surrounds and envelops you, radiating light into all darkness. Feel the pure love of this light permeating your being. As you are touched by this love, you begin to remember your inherent worthiness. You begin to remember that you were born in love, created in the image of the Divine and given physical form as a vessel for your spiritual journey. **2424791 2424797**. Upon this remembrance, you begin to shed all that you have been carrying forth that is out of alignment with this truth. You begin to receive that which you had previously denied. Unconditional love and forgiveness of self flows freely through your being, clearing away all misperceptions and resistance instilled by the ego. **24247247247274 7**. Your heart begins to mirror the sacred heart of the Christ Consciousness, becoming a pure channel for the healing grace of divine love.

Allow conscious awareness of attachment to rise from heart-centered space. Attachment to materialism and monetary wealth. Attachment to unforgiveness, blame, resentment, bitterness or revenge. Attachment to relationships, abuse, the need to be defined by someone else, or loneliness. Attachment to attention, the need to create chaos, to gossip, or the desire to be invisible. Attachment to disease, health, life or death. Allow each to rise to awareness. Attachment leads to suffering and suffering leaves little space for the conscious creation of reality. Visualize all energetic cords and threads holding you bound to attachment. Allow them to be infused with wisdom from the Buddha. As wisdom infuses these cords, they begin to be transmuted into light and love. Release as many cords as possible in this way. **242424247 826242791797 2428242797 7**. Allow the wisdom offered by the Buddha to be interwoven with the love of the Christ consciousness. Breathe this energy into each cell of your being, allowing it be imprinted into your genetic code. **39184248247 3981978917 7**.

Open to receive a red rose from the Divine Mother. Accept it into your heart and nourish it with love and wisdom, bringing it to a full and eternal bloom. Allow this blossoming rose to reawaken the power of the Divine Feminine from within. The feminine and masculine energies within are balancing harmoniously to provide optimal support for your transition. **248247 24624879797 23797971 7 242824247 7**. Place your hand in Hers and begin walking with the Divine Mother. As you glide along crystal paths of rose quartz, allow perceived missteps, throughout the course of your life, to be transmuted and brought into alignment. Walk with Her as she guides you through the crossroads of your life, allowing her to gently correct the energy surrounding each decision that lead you astray. **282621427917 8242 7917**. As these corrections are made, be filled with the understanding that all is well. You are a child of the Divine, growing, learning and evolving, through experiences in physical form, not meant to walk a clear and perfect path. **242628242 7824791797 3 42862425789 7**.

Journey into the crystal core of the center of the Earth. **26426247 837983797 9178247 386428247 7**. Gaia is awaiting your arrival. She honors your presence and willingness to consciously ascend and to assist others along the way. Gaia is nearing the end of her transition into the new grid and is filled with love for the past, present and future and would like to create the space within you for this love to grow. **298247917 2843257984197 6 248248 7**. She is birthing higher consciousness and creating the way for an Earthly reality to be formed with love. She will assist in the initiation of a personal birthing of this consciousness within you, at your request. **26264278262626 3984278247 83917 38427 7 ∞**. Allow her access to your DNA so that she may activate light codes stored within and initiation will begin. **3982424 7 82347 82347 82347 982427 98247 3**.

The current consciousness allows for experiential perception of reality based upon polarity. The recognition of self is realized through the awareness of all that is different from self. Actions are labeled as right or wrong and people are judged as good or bad. In the new grid, consciousness is shifted to the understanding that opposites do not exist, as they are only extreme ends of the spectrum, shifting away from neutral, based on perception. **398247 82497971 7 8247 3 8274**. Allow the polaristic nature of your being to be shifted into oneness. Release the desire to label, judge or separate. All are one, interconnected beyond space, time and the illusion of physical separation. **24824798 24824824798 2 382 4 7**. Surround any resistance to this understanding with an infinity symbol. Offer it up to the sun for transmutation. Fill your heart with green, gold and red light and allow any remaining attachment to polarity to be released. **282624791 7 8242 7 247 8247 7**.

Visualize all obstacles to your path as illusions that dissolve at the casting of conscious awareness upon them. **28648248 2 8247 8917 82487 917 7**. Allow unwavering faith to emanate outward from the core of your being and become a beacon of universal surrender. Set this as your energetic signature, offered to all, through thought, intention and interaction. **28242789187 2 4282478 7 3 6824791 7**. Embrace the ability to move mountains, quench the desert thirst and reap a bountiful harvest from fertile ground. **282 6242879 824791 7 83 4 5862431 7** . Faith lives in the moment and only asks that the still, small voice from within, be heard. Create in accordance with the heart and enjoy the miracle of life. **32 82627912 8 27982 478247 98247 917**.

Spiritual awakening is the cornerstone of creation. **23 8247 8247 8247 328 62419 87 7 ∞**. As you are filled with the knowingness that all you seek lies within, your ability to transcend connection to the old grid, is strengthened. As your heart expands, you see yourself in all others, and all others in yourself. You come to know that separation is an illusion and you refuse to participate in its propagation. There is only you and God, the two, one and the same. In this moment, all barriers to love cease to exist. **28479 8247 18247 7 34824 7 6287 7 7917**. All else, a reflection of the whole, perceived as separate, yet inextricable. **2498247 8247 9179 8 3458247 262 8247 197 7**. Fill your being with green light and offer up your inner child for healing. Return to the innocence of youth, viewing the world with childlike enchantment for the miracle of life. **28247 7 28247 7 6247 8242 7917 7 8242 7917 7**. Breathe deeply and begin to return to conscious awareness. Your attunement is complete.

Chapter 9: Living and Creating from the Heart

Living and creating from the heart requires a different approach than living and creating from the ego or mind. With the ego as your governing authority it was possible to create by sheer force of will, regardless of whether or not what you were trying to create was out of alignment with higher purpose. You could push through and make it happen. When living from the heart, creation is to be in alignment with higher purpose, for your greater good and the greater good of all. There are times, when resistance is harbored, that this prospect can be frustrating; especially when it appears as though you are not getting what you want. The key is in trusting the process, and in knowing that when you do not get what you want, it is because there is something better coming. This "something better" will be subjected to perception. When living from the heart, the blessing in all will be perceived.

Tips and tools to help make the transition out of ego and into heart, with as much ease and grace as possible, follow. Reference these suggestions often and complete the ones which resonate with you. Allow them to see you through difficult times and to assist in the shifting of your perspective.

Bask in Divine Guidance and Assistance

Understand that you are supported on your journey by multifaceted assistance of divine origin. A wonderful way to connect with those who have come to help may be found in stargazing. On clear and cloudless nights, a canopy of stars casts their light upon you, magnifying the wonders of the divine. Know that you are a part of the whole - finite sparks of the infinite.

When the forecast is set to be clear, look up at the stars for twenty minutes. Do this nightly for three nights. Bask in the wonderment of the heavens and know that all is well. There is no limit to what you may create when fortified with the understanding that you are not separate from all that is. All things are possible.

Timing

Understand that timing is everything. Follow up on what inspires you and hold space for aligned connections. Allow your heart to move you, while silencing the ego. As you follow your heart, everything needed falls into place. It is only when falling prey to the ego that fear and lack are permissively expressed.

The Creation Symbol

This symbol for creation was divinely inspired. Use it to saturate your cells with courage and to help release resistance surrounding living from your heart.

Physically: Participate in joyous movement every day. Ten minutes per day will improve brain function, circulation and improve how well you feel. The only requirement is that it be something you enjoy. See Chapter 10 for suggestions to get you started.

Mentally: Release yourself, and others, from expectations. Having attachment to expectations or outcomes is a sure way to make yourself, and others, miserable. It is impossible for you to know the circumstances or context of another human being's thoughts and actions. Because of this, expect nothing, rather allow things to evolve and flow as they will. Kindness to self and others is key. The release of expectations allows for a smooth transition out of ego and into heart.

Embrace change. It's only hard when resisted. Change is going to happen whether or not you approve. Accept things as they are and then take action. Stop fighting. Release weapons of words, actions, and silence. Allow your only defense to be the light of love, radiating outwardly in all directions, from your heart center. This vibration is the only protection you need, as it renders you inaccessible to lower vibrations.

Focus on the common threads that unite neighborhoods, communities, religions, countries and, the world. When focus comes from the heart and is shifted in this direction, peace will reign. Lovingly speak your truth, even when it may not be that of popular opinion. Allow others to do the same. Set intention that every word you speak and every action you take be in accordance with higher purpose and the greater good.

Emotionally: Create and maintain balance in all aspects of your life. Whenever too much time and attention are focused in one area, another area is compromised. Even things you consider to be "good", when done in excess, will disrupt the balance of flow. Consider what deficiencies your ego is attempting to hide through this over-expression. Trust that there is enough time to take care of your family and take care of yourself, to make money and to enjoy recreation and relaxation, to explore your passion and attend to the mundane details of daily life and to be in supportive community and to experience solitude.

Spiritually: Development of a true spiritual connection manifests organically. You cannot bring it into existence by trying and it cannot be forced. You may only create the space within your being to allow this connection to happen. Do this by unplugging from the internet, television, news, video games, etc. Be in nature. Indulge in the silence of solitude.

During this time of solitude, reflect upon your place within nature, within yourself and within your relationships. Are you expressing yourself in the highest way possible? Are you replenishing the earth as the earth nourishes you, by caring for the environment? How could you better care for your planet? Are you treating your body like the wondrous vessel it is for your spirit? How could you better nurture your physical being? Are you taking more than you are giving in relationships? How could you give more freely?

How to Shift in an Instant When Feeling....

Overwhelmed: Visualize yourself within a three dimensional heart. Feel love pouring into your being. Allow the heart to morph into a cube. Feel your energy begin to ground. Watch as the cube morphs into a pyramid. Soak up ancient wisdom. Repeat this sequence eight times or until the feelings of overwhelm have subsided.

Fearful: Place yourself within a sphere, radiating light outwards from every cell of your being. Once the sphere has been filled with this light, realize that there is no room for fear and allow the fear to dissipate. Find yourself filled with the support and strength of your inner mountain. Allow the support and strength to expand. Recognize how powerful your aligned self is. When this power is recognized, your inner mountain is transformed into a bird. You understand that you are free to soar. Repeat this sequence as many times as necessary to release fear.

Sad: Imagine yourself in an egg shaped sea of color. Allow the wind to blow in fuscia to clear visions of the past. They no longer support you, fill them with gratitude and release them. Aqua now fills the space like a soft rain washing away sadness. Violet fills the egg like fire, burning through any remaining sadness. As the fire burns out, your egg of color is filled with green light to bring you back into your heart center. Repeat as many times as necessary to release sadness.

Confused: Visualize five infinity symbols moving throughout your brain. Allow them to sweep away any confusion. Once complete, visualize one infinity symbol connecting your ears, holding one in each loop to maintain clarity.

Chaotic: Stand up and bounce gently on your toes for as long as necessary to shift chaos.

Egoic: Stretch open your chest to clear ego and magnify heart energy.

Resistant: Vigorously shake your entire body for at least one minute to release resistance.

Additionally...

Begin to act with new awareness by recognizing old patterns and identities. Consciously create rather than falling into old ruts at the first sign of trouble. Shine your light brightly into the darkness by awakening to an open heart and allowing others to do the same.

Purify your surrounding environment by decluttering and simplifying. Understand that a chaotic physical environment often results in a chaotic mental and emotional environment. This is a distraction to aligning with the heart.

Solidify your path one step at a time, one person at a time. Life is a journey - not a destination. Focus on the step in front of you and trust that it will take you exactly where you need to be. Trust that the people who come into your life, come for a reason. Identify what they have come to help you learn and joyfully embrace the opportunity.

Be in a supportive community of like minded people walking this journey together. Remember that all are welcome, all are equal and all have a unique contribution to share. Abandon restrictions and judgments. Do not allow them to interfere with your spiritual evolution.

Share your gifts freely from an open heart and without expectation. You are not responsible for the choices another makes; you can only show them an alternate route. The path they ultimately choose is their choice. Allow others to truly see you when you are strong and when you are vulnerable. Remove any masks interfering with how others perceive you in this world. It is safe to be you. It is wonderful to be you!

165

Create and embrace a new reality with every choice you make. Choose to come from love and love will be what you experience. Others will see what you are creating and decide they want to experience love for themselves. You will create the space for that to happen. Create new timelines. Free yourself from old agreements that no longer serve you. Activate new ones that do.

Rejoice! Celebrate all you have created.

 Trudy

Trudy came in on referral for hip and low back pain. Initially our focus was structural, but gradually shifted towards the emotional. We discovered a pattern that whenever Trudy was feeling unsupported, her back would act up. Trudy had been raised to bite her tongue and not to show emotion. Her biggest challenge was to learn how to lovingly speak her truth (and her needs and desires).

She came in for the second retreat and underwent the most dramatic shift I have yet to witness. It is one thing to learn Activating Ascension from a book or to come in for a one-on-one experience. It is entirely different to clear obstacles in group, whether in the context of an Activating Ascension retreat or in a monthly healing circle. Group consciousness combined with intention and technique forms a powerful combination. You will clear more, deeper and faster than would ever be possible through singular means.

In Trudy's case, she was being given the opportunity to find her voice. It was the first time the concept of being corded into oneself was revealed to me. We were about to complete a clearing technique when Trudy began hyperventilating. It was as though she were drowning or being strangled by her fears. She had hundreds of cords that had grown out from her solar plexus and had embedded themselves into and around her throat chakra. Through color, shape, numbers and the use of the blue violet flame she was able to release the cords and free her voice. While the experience was intense, everyone there helped her to hold the space and make the shifts her heart had been longing for.

After the retreat, our focus shifted from finding her voice, to the cultivation of its use for her highest good. She did the hard work, accepting herself and the circumstances she had created. Since then, she retired from her 20 year career and is enjoying the fruits of her labor with her husband from her dream home in the Rockies.

Chapter 10: Mind-Body Purification

Ascension is the rising of consciousness out of ego and into the heart through a strong personal connection to Source, Creator, God. To foster this relationship, your mind and body is to be as free from distraction as possible. Living in a healthy body paves the way for emotional wellness. Emotional wellness is the foundation upon which the relationship with a Higher Power is fostered and cultivated. It is difficult to experience spiritual health if your physical body is in need of purification or your mind is too focused on the mundane details of daily life. A balance is needed. The following recommendations will assist you while transitioning into heart-centered living.

Begin with the preparation phase and transition through all twelve phases at the pace most agreeable to you. Complete, and be prepared to continue, all components in one phase before moving onto the next. If you come upon recommendations that you have already implemented into your daily routine, continue doing so. There is no time frame. Make changes gradually and be kind to yourself throughout. Talk about the changes you are making with friends and family and encourage them to participate. The focus begins predominantly upon the physical body and progresses onto the emotional, mental and spiritual bodies. Reference the quick guide at the end of this chapter, for daily use. Interaction with the *Oracle Activation* Cards begins in Phase IX. While it is not absolutely necessary to use these cards, you will find interaction with them to prove valuable. More information regarding the cards may be found by visiting www.oracleactivationcards.com.

Preparation Phase

Add Fermented Foods and Beverages

Begin adding fermented foods and beverage into your weekly diet. Fermented foods and beverages are high in healthy strains of bacteria that help breakdown and digest foods more completely, thereby increasing the absorption of nutrients. They are also gentle detoxifiers. Fermented beverages include kefir, kombucha, and rejuvelac. These can all be made at home. Kefir and kombucha require a starter culture that can usually be purchased at your local health-food store. Rejuvelac simply requires whole grain cereal or rice. Pickling vegetables and soaking and sprouting nuts and seeds also results in fermentation, creating more of those healthy bacteria. To read more about fermented foods and their health benefits, see Deirdre Rawlings book, *Fermented Foods for Health: Use the Power of Probiotic Foods to Improve your Digestion, Strengthen your Immunity and Prevent Illness.* Many disease processes begin as opportunistic infections that capitalize on imbalances and weakness within the gut and digestive system resulting from diets high in processed foods. Incorporating fermented foods and beverages into your diet creates the opportunity for healing.

Add Superfoods

Superfoods are extremely dense in nutrients. That means they are high in things like antioxidants (believed to slow the aging process), vitamins, minerals, enzymes, fiber and a myriad of immune strengthening phytochemicals that help ward off disease.

At the same time, these foods are low in calories and free of preservatives and other chemicals. Included in this category are: hemp hearts, chia seeds, wheatgrass, raw cacao, goji berries, acai berries, spinach and kale. For more information on superfoods, refer to Carrie May's book, *99 Superfoods*. Incorporate a minimum of three superfoods into your daily diet.

Reduce/Eliminate Processed Soy and Soy Based Foods
Understand that the majority of the American soy crop is genetically modified and is high in pesticide content. Its phytoestrogens may disrupt hormonal balance in both men and women. Soy should not be an exclusive source of protein in any diet. If you would like to keep some amount of soy in your daily routine, stick to fermented sources such as miso, tempeh and natto. Only consume minimally processed and organic sources, in limited moderation.

Reduce Reliance on Animal Based Foods
It is a popular misconception that animal based protein is superior to plant based protein. One can, and many do, eat a vegan diet (free of all animal based foods) and have a balanced intake of protein. The purpose, however, of including this step is not to turn you into a vegan.

Most Americans consume far more protein than necessary. This is putting a significant strain on ecologic systems and the environment. Meat sources reach maturity in half the amount of time it used to take, before they were genetically engineered and otherwise manipulated with growth hormones and other steroids. Their natural diet has been replaced, in large part, by genetically modified foods. Their immune systems have become so compromised that they are consistently pumped with antibiotics. The amount of waste they produce has quadrupled.

All of these changes have resulted in a source of protein that it is more difficult to digest, encourages inflammation and disrupts endocrine function. The most aligned course of action is to buy local and organic sources of meat, raised on their natural diets, free of added hormones and antibiotics and humanely treated. Supplement your diet with high quality vegan sources of protein including green veggies, hemp hearts, nuts, quinoa, lentils and beans.

Phase I

Magnesium
Earlier discussion of magnesium focused on the implications of its deficiency upon intuition development. Additionally, sugar addictions fuel this deficiency as it takes a considerable amount of magnesium to process one molecule of sugar. Do your best to receive as much of your daily requirements from your food, while reducing the amount of added sugar in your diet. Consider filling any gaps with a magnesium supplement. Refer to Chapter 1 for details on daily requirements and bioavailable sources.

Silence
Overstimulation from technology, has many convinced that they must be "plugged in" at all times. It is difficult to cultivate a relationship with the Divine when there is so much interference competing for your attention. It is in silence that the voice of a Higher Power is heard, the personal connection is experienced and the soul is replenished. Regardless of how busy your day is and how many responsibilities you have, commit to fifteen minutes of silence per day.

Fresh Fruit
Eat two servings of fresh (or frozen) fruit daily. Avoid juices and dried fruits, as their sugar content is higher. When fruits are juiced,

fiber is removed and when they are dried, water is removed. Both of these result in consuming more than you would have if you had eaten the whole fruit. While fruit does contain many valuable nutrients, many of them are high in sugar. For the highest benefit and the least amount of sugar, consume blackberries, strawberries and raspberries.

Limit/Eliminate Artificial Sweeteners

Regardless of what is available and how they are marketed, artificial sweeteners are a cocktail of chemical additives that are unrecognizable at the physiological level. They do not stimulate the same area of your brain that natural sugars do, thereby increasing the propensity to over indulge. When your body encounters a compound that it does not know what to do with, it will often wrap it in fat to protect you from it. This process happens with all toxins, including artificial sweeteners. Stick to natural sweeteners such as grade B maple syrup, honey, Yacon syrup and Stevia powder when sweetness is desired. Be aware that most Stevia packets contain maltodextrin, a genetically modified corn product. Always check the ingredients.

Phase II

Omega Three Fatty Acids

Omega three fatty acids play an extremely important role in health. They are necessary for heart and circulatory health, nervous system function, the integrity of hair, skin and nails, digestion and much more. They are also anti-inflammatory, which means they interrupt pain and disease processes. Quality food sources high in omega threes include: flax seeds, walnuts and almonds, fatty fish, avocados, chia seeds, basil and cloves. Currently, there is no official daily recommendation for omega three fatty acids. Aim for 600mg per day. Consider adding a high quality supplement to account for dietary deficiencies.

Astaxanthin

Astaxanthin is an antioxidant made naturally by the body that diminishes free radical formation. Food sources include micro-algea, yeast, krill, salmon and crayfish. As with omega three fatty acids, there is no recommended daily intake for astaxanthin. For optimal functioning, consume between ten and twelve milligrams per day. It is also available in supplement form.

Movement

Move your body a minimum of twenty minutes daily. This does not have to be twenty minutes of intense physical activity. It does need to be something that you enjoy and that generally makes you feel good. Your mind and spirit will thank you immensely. After movement, you will notice an increased ability to see another perspective and to better understand your circumstances. Movement increases blood flow and lymphatic drainage. Movement causes the release of dopamine and serotonin, chemical messengers in the brain that lead to the experience of joy, suppress the appetite, improve coordination and more. Pick a few activities you enjoy, and commit to doing at least one of them for twenty minutes daily. Dancing, walking in nature, playing basketball and/or bouncing on a mini-trampoline are a few options to get you started.

Stretching

After moving your body for twenty minutes, transition into a full body stretch of all major muscle groups. This will help reduce rigidity and improve flexibility within your muscles, as well as within your thoughts. Refer to www.activatingascension.com for a visual presentation of these stretches. Remember, stretching warm muscles reduces likelihood of injury. Hold each stretch for 45-60 seconds. If you experience discomfort or pain within a joint, while stretching, consult a professional for an alternative.

Calves - To stretch the backs of your lower legs, stand with arms extended and pressing against a wall. Come into a shallow lunge position, slightly bending the front knee while extending the back leg and pressing your heel into the floor. Hold and repeat on the other side. While standing in the same position, transition the stretch to the front of the calf by taking the weight off of the heel, extending the ankle and rolling over the toes. Hold and repeat other side.

Hamstrings - To properly stretch the hamstrings, or backs of the thighs, stand with your weight on one foot, knee bent. Extend the other leg out at a 45 degree angle, flex that foot and press the heel into the floor. Maintain the natural curve of your lower back, keep your chest lifted and your neck in a neutral position. Hold and repeat on the other side.

Quadriceps - While standing, shift your weight onto one foot. Reach down with the opposite hand and grasp the ankle, allowing the knee to bend and the foot to come towards your bottom. Keep knees close together and flex the foot for a deeper stretch felt on the front of your thigh. Hold and repeat on the other side.

Hip Flexors - These muscles are located along the front of the hips. Come into a lunge position, making sure that the forward knee does not jut out over the toe. Lift your chest to vertical, raise arms overhead, maintaining your neck in a neutral position. Sink the pelvis towards the floor, lengthening the front of the hip. Hold and repeat on the other side.

Side Body - Your iliotibial bands are located along the outsides of your thighs. Their tightness is a common cause of knee pain as they cause an uneven force on the kneecap. Your quadratus lombori are muscles of the low back, important in stabilizing the pelvis, and are often implicated in low back pain. Your latissimus dorsi are the biggest back muscles, contributing to the "V" shaped back of athletes and those that regularly weight train. They can all be stretched together in one movement.

Stand and cross your right foot over your left. Raise arms overhead and grasp your left wrist with your right hand. Shift weight onto the left foot and allow your hips to come out to the left. While keeping your hips and shoulders square, pull your left arm overhead and to the right. Keep your arms back by your ears and maintain your neck in a neutral position. This stretch opens the entire side of the body. Hold and repeat on the other side.

Chest - While standing, clasp hands behind the body, extend arms and raise them until a deep stretch is felt in the chest. Maintain a neutral neck position.

Back - With arms extended to the front, cross right arm over left and bring the palms of your hands together. Maintain neck in a neutral position and hold.

Shoulders - Stand with your weight evenly distributed. Bring your right arm across your body at shoulder height. Pull your upper arm across your body with your left hand and rotate the palm outward to deepen the stretch. Hold and repeat on the other side.

Biceps - Stand, facing away from a wall. Reach your right arm back, wrist externally rotated and palm pressing against the wall. Rotate shoulders away to stretch the front of your upper arms. Hold and repeat on the other side.

Triceps - Extend right arm over head allowing the elbow to flex. Pull back on the right arm at the elbow with the left hand, keeping the right arm close to the ear and the neck in neutral. This stretch will be felt in the back of the upper arm. Hold and repeat on the other side.

Wrists - Extend right arm out in front, palm facing up. Use your left hand to gently pull the right hand into extension to stretch the inside of the lower arm and front of wrist. Rotate palm down and repeat to stretch the outside of the lower arm and back of the wrist. Hold each position and repeat on the other side.

Neck - Bring right hand overhead, to just above left ear. Apply a gentle pull so that your right ear comes closer to your right shoulder. At the same time, reach towards the floor with your left hand to deepen the stretch along the left side of the neck. To transfer the stretch to the back of your neck, rotate your chin towards your right underarm and shift the line of pull of your right hand to slightly behind the head on the left side. Hold each position and repeat on the other side.

Limit/Eliminate Monosodium Glutamate and Other Chemical Additives

Monosodium glutamate, commonly known as MSG, is toxic to the nervous system. It can cause headaches and other allergic reactions. Lab tests have shown that it causes rats to gain weight that they are then unable to lose. As with other chemical additives and compounds that are unrecognizable to your digestive system, your body spends a lot of energy trying to figure out what to do with them and may ultimately store them within adipose cells. Diligently read labels and inquire about the use of MSG and other additives in restaurants. Foods that do not include MSG in the ingredients are often labeled as MSG free.

Phase III

Hydrate

Many common symptoms including headaches, lethargy, forgetfulness and irritability can be a result of dehydration. Many operate at less than optimal levels of hydration in their daily lives. Sometimes excuses are made to rationalize symptoms as having a more dramatic cause than dehydration. The solution to your symptom may really be this simple.

A great rule of thumb to consider is to drink half your bodyweight, in ounces, of water, daily. If you are an athlete or participate in vigorous physical activity, it is likely that you are losing more water than the average person. Weigh yourself before and after training and drink at least one pint of water for every pound lost. Also, when participating in strenuous physical activity, you should sweat. Sweating is how your body regulates its temperature. The inability to sweat is a sign of imbalance in need of further evaluation.

Now that you know how much water to drink, consider your water source. Carrying around disposable plastic water bottles has become the norm for many. These bottles are causing a huge strain on the environment as it takes an astronomical amount of time for them to degrade, if they ever do. Also, these soft water bottles contain a compound called bis-phenol A, or BPA. This chemical leaks out into the water and results in a gradual increase in plastic toxicity in those who drink it.

Tap water is readily available, though it is often fluoridated (as previously discussed in Chapter 1). It also contains impurities such as arsenic, lead and trace amounts of prescription medications. The authorities governing water treatment facilities are not always aligned with the greater good. Research your cities water sources and treatment procedures to make an informed decision. If you have access to well water, have it tested for contents.

Consider investing in a water filtration system. Understand that fluoride is an extremely small molecule and requires special equipment to filter it out. Before purchasing any system, ensure that it includes fluoride removal. Whole house systems are available as are smaller variations that attach to the kitchen faucet. There are also standalone and portable systems that can be used to filter and purify water.

Distilled water is another option. Be aware that the distillation process removes all minerals and electrolytes from the water and that they will need to be added prior to consumption.

Eat Beets
While not everyone's favorite vegetable, beets are a nutrient dense energy source. They gently detoxify the liver, boost mental health, improve libido and are packed with many vitamins and minerals. They can be pickled, eaten raw or roasted. They have an earthy flavor, but don't let that deter you. Experiment with different recipes and you will easily find one you like. Include them in your diet on a weekly basis.

Be in Nature
Communion with nature brings one closer to the Divine while energetically grounding them into the Earth simultaneously. Walk outside barefoot, lay on the ground, dig in the dirt with your bare hands. Listen to the birds, feel the wind and soak up the sun. This time will revitalize and renew your energies. It will also help replenish your vitamin D stores, which get low in the winter time while its production is inhibited due to sunscreen use in the summer. Be in nature for twenty minutes per day.

Limit/Eliminate High Fructose Corn Syrup

Contrary to what manufacturers would like you to believe, the chemical structure of high fructose corn syrup is unrecognizable as corn. It is much cheaper than cane sugar and has replaced cane sugar as a sweetener in almost every instance. It cannot be labeled as organic, because it is not. Lab studies have shown that cancer cells replicate twice as fast in a high fructose corn syrup medium when compared with regular sugar. It is not beneficial for you, even in moderation. Check your labels and you will be amazed at how ubiquitous this product is. Begin removing it from your diet now.

Phase IV

Think and Speak Consciously

To paraphrase Gandhi, choose your thoughts wisely, for they become your words, which govern your actions and create your reality. Become aware of negative thoughts and self-talk that feed false beliefs conjured by the ego. This awareness will help you shift out of the pattern and reduce the amount of energy that feeds them. Over time and with this deprivation of energy, the voices that speak to you from a place of less than love, will cease to exist because you stopped listening.

Eat Your Veggies

Consistently eat three servings of vegetables every day. Fresh and in-season are optimal, followed by frozen. Avoid canned vegetables whenever possible, unless they have been canned via traditional homesteading means. Even the cans of organic brands may be lined with a material that contains BPA. Stick with colorful veggies. You can eat corn and white potatoes, but do not count them towards your daily goal of three servings. Eat as many of them as possible in their raw state, or lightly steamed. Consider planting a garden or participating in a local CSA (Community Supported Agriculture) program.

Listen to Music
Listen to 30 minutes of high vibrational music daily. This music allows an effortless shift into heart space. Play it in the background as you begin your day or over dinner. Classical music, nature CDs and healing CDs offer abundant variety from which to choose. Only listen to that which resonates with your heart and causes your soul to smile.

Limit/Eliminate Fat Free or Reduced Fat Food Products
Understand that whenever you see these labels, it usually means that something that was naturally included was removed and replaced with artificial chemicals and additives. Fats, as they naturally occur, are a healthy and necessary nutrient. Fat is used for energy and is also responsible for the chemical signal that tells your brain that you are full. It is usually replaced with high fructose corn syrup or artificial sweeteners that do not send this signal to the brain. The result is that you end up eating more of the reduced or fat free version than you would have, had you eaten the regular version.

Phase V

Reduce Dietary Gluten
Gluten is the protein found in barley, rye and wheat (including: spelt, kamut, durum, farro, bulgar and semolina) and is responsible for the elastic texture of dough. It is found in most breads, crackers, cereals and pastries. Gluten causes a mucosal covering to form within the small intestine that may make it difficult to absorb other nutrients. For example, vitamins and minerals from other nutrient dense foods or from supplements you may be taking may not be absorbed due to the presence of this covering.

Celiac disease is caused by an immune reaction to gluten in some people. In people without celiac, the response to gluten is less severe and may be labeled a sensitivity or intolerance. Blood tests check for several reactions indicating that gluten intolerance may be present. Keep in mind that blood tests are only positive when enough of a reaction is taking place to be considered clinical. It seems as though you go to sleep one night, processing gluten perfectly and then wake up the next day to discover that you have sensitivity to gluten. In truth, the breakdown in the ability to effectively process gluten has been building over years, even decades.

In this phase, begin reducing the amount of gluten containing foods in your diet by 40%. You will begin to notice an increase in energy and vitality almost immediately. An added benefit may be the release of unwanted weight. Do not replace all of the gluten containing foods you've been eating with gluten free versions. These options are typically no better for you than their gluten containing counterpart. Consider experimenting with alternate grains such as amaranth, millet, buckwheat and quinoa. Above all, listen to your body. If you notice overall improvements to your health and well being by simply reducing the amount of grains consumed, don't be in a hurry to replace them. It may be that your body operates optimally on a diet low in grains.

Eat Brussels Sprouts
Brussels sprouts are cruciferous vegetables that resemble little cabbages. They are packed with protein, fiber, vitamins, minerals and antioxidants. They, along with beets, help to gently detoxify and cleanse your liver. Eat them once per week.

Reduce Sugar Intake

Sugar is a key ingredient in almost every disease process known to man. It feeds bacterial, viral, fungal and parasitic infections, as it provides the perfect environment for their reproduction and perpetuates their presence. Cancer cells also thrive in this culture. Sugar causes inflammation, leading to scarring of vascular tissues (which is then patched by cholesterol) paving the way for atherosclerosis and heart disease. This same inflammation feeds joint stiffness and arthritic pain. Sugar may also cause "brain fog", confusion and forgetfulness. Degenerative disease patterns are slowed, and oftentimes even reversed, when sugar is removed from the diet.

Regrettably, the society in which you live is inundated with sugar. In all its many forms, it is used to celebrate, to mourn and to numb emotional pain. Sugar is often used to fill an emotional void. Instead, be sweeter and kinder to yourself in other ways. Developing a conscious connection with a Higher Power will assist in reclaiming the power given to sugar. Cultivating loving relationships, displaying fresh flowers, and slowing down are all ways to be sweeter to yourself.

Begin reducing dietary intake of sugar to a **maximum of 35 grams per day**. Yes, this does include fruit sugar as well as processed sugars. While it is important to eat two servings of fresh fruit each day, it is equally important not to eat more than two servings. Focus on fruits from the berry family, which are naturally lower in sugar. Read all labels as sugar is often added to foods least expected. Do your best and forgive yourself the rest.

Limit/Eliminate Table Salt

NaCl is the chemical compound known as table salt. It is highly refined and processed and disrupts the body's biochemistry; leading to things like high blood pressure and other disease processes. Regular table salt is often fortified with Iodine, a trace mineral necessary for a healthy metabolism. Unfortunately, iodine competes with and often loses to chloride (the Cl part of NaCl) at receptor sites. Many processed foods and most restaurant foods are loaded with sodium. Eat at home as often as possible and replace table salt with sea salt. Sea salt is salt in its natural state that is unprocessed and loaded with trace minerals. It does not have the negative effects on metabolism and blood pressure associated with table salt. High quality sea salt is typically pink or grey.

Phase VI

Improve Digestion

Digestive enzymes are made by your body to assist in the proper digestion and absorption of carbohydrates and proteins. For various reasons, over time the production of these compounds slows and additional help may be required. If you have issues with constipation or diarrhea, gas or bloating, or acid reflux, it is likely that you will benefit from eating foods that assist in digestion or by adding a digestive enzyme supplement.

You implemented the addition of fermented foods and beverages in the preparation phase and those healthy bacterial strains have been hard at work repairing weak spots throughout your digestive tract. It is likely that improved digestion has already been noted. For a greater impact, consider the following. There are several spices, including mustard, garlic and cayenne, that stimulate salivary glands and encourage the release of digestive enzymes. Peppermint, ginger and fennel are among the many herbs that help to cleanse and release toxins through their gentle laxative effect. The acid content of lemons help the body absorb more calcium and breakdown proteins more effectively. You may want to consider adding a broad spectrum digestive enzyme or hydrochloric acid supplement for additional support.

Epsom Salt Baths

Magnesium sulphate, commonly known as Epsom salts, has many beneficial properties. The magnesium content helps to sooth sore or stiff muscles. It also helps to rid the body of negativity. If baths are not your preference, the salt can be massaged into the belly and sore muscles while in the shower. Or, soak in a foot bath. Add a 20 minute Epsom salt bath or foot soak into your routine, once per week

Release Anger, Bitterness and Vengefulness

These are some of the ego's favorite tools to maintain the illusion of separation. They serve no one, least of all the person harboring them. It has been proven that these emotions stress the body to the extent that they compromise the immune system. Lowered immunity opens the door to opportunistic infections and other disease processes. These emotions also significantly lower the amount of joy you are able to experience and the level of happiness you are able to create in each moment. Once the realization is made that it is only yourself that is hurt by harboring these emotions, you are able to release them.

Practice the anger release technique daily, and hold the intention that the bitterness and vengefulness goes with it. Intuit an energy routine to further support your intentions for release. Consider releasing with breath, a number activation sequence, color, sound, shape, etc. It requires a great deal of energy to fuel these emotions. You will be amazed at how much better you feel and how much more you are able to accomplish without them.

Be in Supportive Community
Whether it is in religious affiliation, in your neighborhood or, perhaps in a like minded social group, make efforts to be in supportive community on a weekly basis. This community should support, encourage and empower one another to live in the heart, free from fear, with conscious realization of connection. The members of the community should nourish each other and readily share their gifts and wisdom. The focus should be on the positive and on ways to bring more love into the world while understanding common needs: a desire to be heard, to be accepted, to be loved, to be forgiven, to live in peace, to experience abundance, and more.

Phase VII

Coenzyme Q10
Coenzyme Q10, or CoQ10, is a necessary component for energy production at a cellular level. Your body makes it naturally on a somewhat limited basis. The rest of it comes from food or a CoQ10 supplement. Foods rich in the enzyme include: coldwater fish (tuna, salmon, mackerel and sardines), grass fed beef, organic chicken, avocados, sesame seeds and spinach. Animal sources definitely contain higher amounts. Another option would be to add a quality CoQ10 supplement. There is no established recommended level. Aim for a minimum of 30 mg per day.

Frivolous Fun
Schedule daily time for frivolous fun. It is a common misperception that you have to be productive every moment of the day. Quiet the ego and cultivate your inner light through playful interaction. Sing, dance, fingerpaint, make funny faces, play in the rain, play with your kids, play with your pets. Repeat, daily.

Transition into the Heart
Consciously begin to shift your attention/intention from your ego to your heart. Really feel this connection before moving on to the next. Be willing to complete this shift as soon as you realize you've slipped out of your heart. With this shift, a new biochemical environment of neurotransmitters will be created. Old connections that held you back will be released and new connections that will support you in your journey will be created. You will soon discover that this is where you are meant to be. In this place, you are free, you are home.

Limit/Eliminate Food Dyes and Colorings
Many popular food dyes and colorings are linked to things like hyperactivity, allergic reactions and decreased immune response. All of which act as distractions from the relationship we are trying most to cultivate. Avoid ingesting them whenever possible. They are clearly labeled on packaged foods. If using them to colors eggs or in other crafts, wear gloves to protect against absorption.

Phase VIII

30% Raw
The cooking process downgrades and denatures proteins and enzymes in otherwise nutrient dense foods. This includes the pasteurization process of dairy products and other liquids. Begin consuming 30% of your calories from raw foods. If you are regularly eating salads and fresh fruits, this practice has likely already been implemented. Avoiding boredom from eating the same foods over and over is key to maintaining the course. Consult with raw food books and research recipes to avoid this. Consider investing in a quality high-speed blender and dehydrator to add variety. The benefits of eating more raw foods include slowing the aging process, more energy and greater clarity.

Practice Forgiveness

When the word forgiveness is mentioned, your first thoughts may drift to people in your life who have hurt you in some way or another. The ego outwardly directs attention to fulfill the desire to blame others rather than to look inward and bring healing to the hurt. Blaming others absolves you from acknowledging your role in what happened, allowing you to relish in self-pity and obscure your vision from moving forward in new ways. It is only yourself that is punished by withholding forgiveness from others. Begin by forgiving yourself and then extend forgiveness to others.

Use Activating Ascension and begin releasing all that lies heavily upon your heart. Your Higher Power does not keep score or lay blame, but is only pure love waiting to welcome you with open arms. Set aside time to do this weekly. It doesn't take much; an open heart and a willingness to forgive is all that is required.

Volunteer

In Phase VI you committed to regularly being in supportive community. Take what you have learned and begin sharing the wisdom and insights you have gained throughout this journey. Volunteer to help others. In helping others, the space is created to relieve your heart from the constraints of ego. Choose to volunteer in whatever way you feel drawn. Share your open heart with others by being of service and in being present. Commit to one hour per week.

You may want to research volunteer opportunities in your neighborhood, religious organization or local hospital. Or, take the less formal route and simply ask a neighbor or friend if they could use some extra help or know someone that does. It doesn't have to be complicated. You will be rewarded for your efforts through rejuvenation of your spirit.

Limit/Eliminate Caffeine

Caffeine can be a drain to your nervous system. When consumed in excess, it perpetuates your need for it by disrupting the sleep cycle and sending your adrenals, or stress glands, into overdrive. Attempting to eliminate caffeine all at once may elicit withdrawal symptoms. Gradually reduce consumption until patterns of addiction have been released. For instance, if you are currently drinking five caffeinated beverages per day, reduce it by two. Allow your body to adjust to the decreased amount over the next two weeks. Make further reductions in the same manner until you are able to eliminate caffeine completely. Occasional consumption of caffeine, unaccompanied by addiction, will not significantly interfere with ascension.

 Melissa

Melissa was referred to me by a massage therapist for decreased right shoulder mobility. She suspected it was associated with emotional stress, as physical manipulation was not eliciting improvement. When she came in for her initial visit and interview, I learned that her son had been diagnosed with an extremely aggressive form of testicular cancer at age 22. We set the primary objective for her care to restore structural integrity to her neck and right shoulder with the priorities of developing acceptance of and detachment from the cycle of life and the release of fear. When she returned from her report of findings, this is what she had to say:

"After the energetic balancing we did during the Initial Visit, I felt great and slept better than I have since before this whole thing started. My husband said I slept so soundly that he was worried I

had taken two tramadol instead of one. I told him that I didn't take any and haven't needed any to sleep since. I'm ready, let's get started!"

Since then, they learned that their son is terminal and that there is nothing further to be done. Even so, Melissa's sleep continues to improve. Though we have not directly treated her neck and shoulder, her range of motion continues to improve, while pain is decreasing. She is able to engage in life and enjoy her family. Melissa is preparing for the next evolution of her career and has been able to decrease the amount of stress in her life even further by giving herself permission to cease all unnecessary communication with her ex-husband.

Phase IX

Help Others

Offer your help whenever possible. Empower. Educate. Assist. Never push, force or go where you are unwanted. Those who may most benefit by what you have to share will cross your path. Some will be ready and willing. Focus on them. Plant seeds in the unwilling and hold the intention that they will be watered over time.

Glutathione

Glutathione is the body's most powerful and naturally occurring antioxidant. It boosts the immune systems, is integral to repair of damaged tissues caused by inflammation, and aids in detoxification. Production of glutathione decreases with age. You can help facilitate its production by eating foods that contain its building blocks. Examples include okra, rosemary, curry, kale and broccoli. You may also consider adding a glutathione supplement. While it is preferable to receive nutrients from food, supplementation helps bridge gaps of deficiency.

Heart Opening and Nourishment **Oracle Activation Cards**
Begin looking at the Heart Opening and Nourishment cards in sequence, twice per week. Look at each for a moment before moving on to the next. Set your intention for heart opening and reception of nourishment and allow the images to do the rest. This will strengthen your alignment and relationship with your Higher Power.

Limit/Eliminate Microwaved Foods
Microwaving considerably reduces the amount and quality of nutrients in food. You have probably already significantly reduced how many microwaved foods you are eating, as you have implemented prior changes. Continue this reduction until they have been completely eliminated. Use alternatives like a toaster oven or a conventional oven to reheat foods. Microwaves also lower the vibration of water; use a traditional or electric teapot to heat water for tea.

Phase X

40% Raw
Continue increasing caloric intake from raw fruits and vegetables. Consume seeds and nuts in moderation and in accordance with your body's ability to digest them. Appreciate improved energy levels as the requirements for digestion are decreased and this newly freed energy is redirected elsewhere.

Journal
Begin keeping a daily journal. Something magical happens in the process of transferring your thoughts into written words. Write down whatever is on your mind at the time. Cast no judgment upon the words. You will notice that you sleep better whenever your thoughts are put on paper and unable to relentlessly run

through your mind. Journaling will also help you gain a better perspective, inspire creative solutions and release confusion.

Limit/Eliminate Alcohol

Alcohol is in the same group with caffeine and sugar when it comes to adverse effects on wellbeing, when over consumed or associated with addiction. It is a depressant and does limit one's ability to be fully present. It is often used as an escape. As you have gone through this process you have learned how to create a natural high without the use of alcohol. You participate in daily forms of frivolous fun, enjoy being uplifted and uplifting others through supportive community, and take meticulous care of your physical body. Your heart is open and you understand that loving yourself is a choice to be made in every moment. Alcohol inhibits the flow of this energy and lowers your vibration, making you an easy target for fear. Begin eliminating it now.

Reduce Sugar Intake

Further reduce sugar intake to a maximum of 25 grams per day. You are kind and sweet to yourself and share and receive kindness and sweetness with and from others. This is the last reduction of sugar consumption to be made.

Phase XI

Sing from your Heart

This is slightly different from frivolous fun. Participating in activities that elicit your heart song has a deeper meaning and purpose for fulfillment and passion. If you are currently in a career that deprives your senses, start exploring new opportunities. Use the Activating Ascension protocol to clear anything stopping you from doing so. When your heart is open and allowing your divine will to be done, the perfect career opportunity will become available. Until a transition can be made, engage in hobbies you've loved since childhood or take up a new one. Don't know what you like to do? Experiment. Take a class, sign up for a workshop, talk with others about what they love to do and how they got started. Hobbies often evolve into fulfilling careers. It is not work when it elicits joy.

Release Your Inner Judge

In releasing yourself from judgment, the space and freedom to love yourself is created. When you are free to love yourself, then you are free to love others and release them from judgment as well. Acceptance of oneself is evidenced by one's ability to accept another exactly as they are, not as the ego may wish them to be. This is the last major obstacle in surrendering the ego and ascending into the heart.

Further Gluten Reduction

Reduce amount of gluten containing foods remaining by 60%. You are already feeling so good at this point, this reduction will come easily.

Limit/Eliminate Genetically Modified Foods

The subject of genetically modified foods was mentioned earlier. It would be optimal if the governing body regulating the safety of your food supply was in alignment with the greater good. Sadly, they are heavily influenced by monetary gains and special interest groups. Do not rely on them to provide truthful information regarding genetically modified foods and the processes that create them. Ten of the most commonly genetically modified foods are: sugar beets, potatoes, corn, tomatoes, squash, golden rice, soybeans, canola oil, animal feed and salmon.

Buying food that is labeled "USDA Certified Organic" or from a trusted local farmer are two ways to ensure your food is GMO free. Genetically modified produce, when labeled with the optional

PLU (price look up number), has a five digit code beginning with the number 8. A four digit code signifies conventionally grown produce and a five digit code beginning with the number 9 designates foods that have been organically grown. There are currently no requirements for food manufacturers to label genetically modified foods. Buying organic provides a degree of security, as genetically modified foods cannot be labeled as organic.

Note: If you would like to know more about your food source, consider viewing the following documentaries: *Food Inc.; Fresh; Fat, Sick and Nearly Dead; Forks Over Knives; King Corn;* and *Ingredients.*

Phase XII

50% Raw
Increase the amount of calories consumed from raw food sources to 50%. This is the final increase, though you may choose to further transition into a raw foods diet. Some will do extremely well on a 100% raw diet, while others will not. Tune-in and ask your body what it needs to function optimally and follow your intuition.

Heart Opening and Nourishment Oracle Activation Cards
Look at the Light Body Activation and Nourishment cards in sequence as often as you are called. View each image for 3-4 seconds. Allow the frequencies from the cards to access and activate your heart center continuously. Know that you will be passively sharing these activations with all who cross your path.

Conscious Connection with Source
Be consciously connected with Source in every moment and watch as your everyday life is transformed into the miraculous.

Start an Activating Ascension Study Group
Take an active role in supportive community. Start an Activating Ascension study group where members come together to clear blocks and support each other throughout the process. Clearing in group settings clears deeper and much faster than when clearing individually. For more information on how to start such a group visit www.activatingascension.com.

Mind-Body Purification: Recap

Preparation Phase
Add Fermented Foods and Beverages
Add Superfoods
Reduce/Eliminate Processed Soy and Soy Based Foods
Reduce Reliance on Animal Based Foods

Phase I
Magnesium
Silence
Fresh Fruit (2 Servings)
Limit/Eliminate Artificial Sweeteners

Phase II
Omega Three Fatty Acids
Astaxanthin
Movement
Stretching
Limit/Eliminate Monosodium Glutamate and Other Chemical Additives

Phase III
Stay Hydrated
Eat Beets
Be in Nature
Limit/Eliminate High Fructose Corn Syrup

Phase IV
Think and Speak Consciously
Veggies
Listen to Music
Limit/Eliminate Fat Free or Reduced Fat Food Products

Phase V
Reduce Dietary Gluten
Eat Brussels Sprouts
Reduce Sugar Intake
Limit/Eliminate Table Salt

Phase VI
Improve Digestion
Epsom Salt Baths
Release Anger, Bitterness and Vengefulness
Be in Supportive Community

Phase VII
Coenzyme Q10
Frivolous Fun
Transition into the Heart
Limit/Eliminate Food Dyes and Colorings

Phase VIII
30% Raw
Practice Forgiveness
Volunteer
Limit/Eliminate Caffeine

Phase IX
Help Others
Glutathione
Heart Opening and Nourishment Cards
Limit/Eliminate Microwaved Foods

Phase X
40% Raw
Journal
Limit/Eliminate Alcohol
Reduce Sugar Intake

Phase XI
Make Your Heart Sing
Release Your Inner Judge
Further Gluten Reduction
Limit/Eliminate Foods Containing Genetically Modified Organisms

Phase XII
50% Raw
Heart Opening and Nourishment Cards
Start an Activating Ascension Study Group
Conscious Connection with Source

Appendix A: Activating Ascension
~ Step-by-Step ~

Find a quiet space, breathe deeply and become centered.

1. Open sacred circlc

2. Establish a pure connection

3. Come into your Sacred Heart

4. Set your intention or say a prayer

5. Radiate creation energy

6. Open to Divine guidance

7. Connect with your assistance

8. Intuitively determine the number of agendas

9. Identify and record each agenda

10. Intuit the number of initial aspects for each agenda

11. Identify how many and which obstacles make up each agenda

12. Identify how many and which techniques will be needed to clear each agenda

13. Complete the techniques

14. Intuit the number of remaining aspects

15. Fill the void

16. Request integration

17. Ask how long it's going to take to process this session and make note of it

18. Determine date of next session

19. Ask if there are additional agendas for this intention and, if so, how many more

20. Determine follow up

21. Consider what steps are to be taken as part of your action plan

22. Offer the healing you completed to anyone who may benefit from it

23. Give thanks and close your sacred circle

Appendix B
Activating Ascension: Tools Table Part I

Assistance	Agenda	Level I Clearing Techniques	Level II Clearing Techniques
Guardian Angels Holy Spirit Guides	Physical Symptoms (Pains, Headaches, digestion issues, poor sleep, fatigue, weight, etc.)		**Active** Power reclamation Re-assimilation of disowned selves Aligning with your highest path
Archangels (Raphael, Michael, Uriel, Jophiel, Sandalphon, Ariel, Chamuel, Gabriel,	Fear (generalized, of the unknown, of moving forward, of succeeding, of failing, of the future, of the past, of change, of commitment, of being wrong, of finishing, repercussions, rejection, of asking the wrong questions, of missing the point, of asking for help, of not being enough, of leaving loved ones behind, etc)	Switching, Grounding Energy Therapy, Resistance Release, Breath Release, Prayer, Fear Release, Anger Release Movement, Sound, Shapes, Colors, DNA Restoration, DNA Reconfiguration Nervous System Balancing, Energetic Remedies	Number Activation Sequences: Heart, Blending old self with new self, In your body, Transition Mask Removal Holding your own space Washing away misperceptions Implant Removal Grid building for creation Merging Energy Streams:
Ascended Masters (Jesus, Mother Mary, Buddha, Quan Yin, Kuthumi, Mahatma, etc.) Saints (Mary Magdalene, Joan of Arc, Theresa of Lisieux, Mother Theresa, Padre Pio, etc.)	Relationships (romantic, familial, friendly, occupational, self, etc.) Career (dream job, fulfillment, purpose, advancement, sabotage, expertise, security, etc.)	12 Rays of God, Erasing Mental Matrices Number Activations, Positive Imprinting Clearing Field, Easing Pain, Creating Wholeness, Activating Impulses,	Familial, Environmental, Creation, Forgotten, Cooperation, Dimensional, World, Past Life **Passive** Energy Balancing: Heart, brain, reproductive system
Nature (Faeries, sprites, devas, pan, the 4 directions, the sun, moon, and stars, animals, crystals and stones, the five elements, elementals, etc.)	Overall Happiness (love, peace, joy, passion, vitality, contentment, playfulness, fun, motivation, creativity) Finances (releasing debt, accepting wealth, worthy of wealth, fiscal responsibility, alignment)	Contract Dissolution, Dissolving the Old Grid, Separation of Energy Fields, Increasing Intuition, Programming Discs, Releasing Resentment, Habits and Addictions, Bringing Love, GPR	Adrenal Reset Rings of fire Central Nervous System Release Reproductive System Cleansing Balancing the time/space continuum Battery Recharge Divine Connections (3) Pain Relief Sequence Heart Opening Sequence
Interdimensional Beings	Disconnection from normalcy, Desire to just get by, Acceptance Missing Big Picture Detach from story Atonement, Other	Spirit Release Cards	

Appendix B
Activating Ascension: Tools Table Part I (cont'd.)

Follow Up	Supplements/ Homeopathics	Reactions to Release	Action Plan
Mental: Learn something new, rest, stay connected, ground. Emotional: Cry, laugh, hug, journal, play, allow and receive. Physical: Dance, walk, skip, jump, run. Dietary changes. Rest/Sleep, Breathe Spiritual: Pray, meditate, spend time in nature, tone, ohm, chant, be in supportive community. Misc.: Hydrate, do not take yourself so seriously, release attachment, revisit intentions, observe changes. Massage, Energy Session, Other See the Supplement/Homeo pathic column	Supplements: CoQ10, fatty acids, glutathione, probiotics, wheatgrass Vitamins: A, B, C, D, E, K Protomorphogens: Kidney, adrenal, liver, pancreas, thyroid, heart, lungs, spleen, pituitary, hypothalamus Minerals: Calcium, Magnesium, Molybdeum, Selenium, Manganese, Potassium, Iodine Homeopathics: Argentum Nitricum (fear), Ignatia Amara (grief), Oscillococcinum (cold/flu), Carnelia Sinensis (sleep, digestion) Essential Oils Flower Essences Other	Fatigue Achiness Anger Anxiety Confusion Sadness Resentment Intestinal Discomfort Lowered Immunity Short Circuiting of the CNS Peace Happiness Joy/Love Feeling Free Irritation Other	Revisit something you tried in the past to achieve your intention. Seek expert assistance. Seek support. Talk to others who have already achieved a similar intention. Expand your knowledge. Support others. Vision board, affirmations, mantras, see your goal realized. Other

201

Appendix B
Activating Ascension: Tools Table Part II Obstacles

Emotions	Past Life	Experience	Consciousness Pattern	Triggers
Fear	Misuse of	Traumatic	Martyr	Lied to
Anger	power	(accidents,		
Rage/Fury	Attachment	abuse, rape,	Victim	Manipulated
	Betrayal	loss, etc.)		
Sadness			Warrior	Authority
Depression	Maintaining	Left out,		
Disappoint-	the status quo	cheated,	People Pleaser	Judgment
ment		chastised,		
Exhaustion	Community:	Stopped by	Addict	Being
	abandonment,	fear, Let down,		controlled
Remorse	starvation,		Liar	
Guilt	enslavement,	Accepted		Being
Hatred	exiling, etc.)	other peoples	Needy	looked
Blame		beliefs or		down upon
	Familial	opinions as	Turned Off	
Shame	Issues (loss of	truth		Rejection
Irritation	loved one,		Other	
Frustration	abuse, war,	Taken		Other
	betrayal,	advantage of,		
Competition	abandonment,	Blindsided or		
Insecurity	etc.)	caught off		
Jealousy		guard		
Resentment	Religious			
Annoyance	persecution	Subjugated,		
	Traumatic	refused,		
Confusion	death	rejected,		
Anxiety		domesticated		
Revenge	Other			
		Other		
Other				

Appendix B
Activating Ascension: Tools Table Part II Obstacles (cont'd.)

Behaviors	Inherited Beliefs	False Mental Matrices	Completed Contracts	Misc.
Aggressive Argumentative	You have to work hard to make money.	I am ugly/fat/ dumb/stupid/ not good enough/ never going to amount to anything/I am unworthy/ unclean /tainted/unacceptable as I am/I am useless/ thoughtless /clueless/an idiot/ too old	Poverty	Mis-understanding
Bossy Controlling Domineering			Silence	Misinterpreting
	Good things happen to other people.		Celibacy	Misdiagnosis
Needy Addictions Deceitful			Servitude	Wrong Prescription
			Obedience	
Inconsiderate/ Thoughtless Irritating	Money is a measure of personal worth.	There is not enough. I can't. I am unlovable.	Being less than	Misaligned
			Resisting Divinity	Outside of Allowance
Mania Depression	You are too weak.	If I succeed others will hate me. Everyone is out to get me.	Denying Mastery	Untouchable
Unsure, Timid Shy, Naïve	Life is hard.		Illness	Fell for the Illusion
Manipulative Moody Rude/Spiteful	You don't deserve ____.	To be free means to be separate.	Relationships	
			Sabotage	
Too Nice, Unbalanced, audacious, limp	You have to do it all by yourself.	The world is bad/ dangerous/scary. It's doomed anyway I don't want to	Interdimen-sional Agreements	
Other	You can't ____.	I don't belong Change is hard Other.	Other	
	Things can't be changed. It's bad to be different. Other			

Activating Ascension Sessi(

Prayer

Open Circle → Pure Connection → Sacred Heart _____ Radiate -
Energy
Intention

Agendas (Numl

_____ _____   _____
(   )   (   )

Obstacles

Techniques

Remaining
# of Aspects: (   )   (

Fill the void → Processing Time: _____ → Next Session Date: _____→ Follow Up: _
Request Integration   # Of additional Agendas for   (Note how
                               this intention: _____   much and ⁻
                                                                      for how ⁻
                                                                       long) ⁻

Appendix C (cont'd.)

ɔn Guide

Name: _____
Date: _____

_____

→ Open to Divine → Assistance: _____ → #of Agendas ___
   Guidance   _____

ɔer of Aspects):

_____   _____
                              (   )

)   (   )

_____ → Reactions: _____ → Action Plan: _____

_____   _____
_____   _____   Offer Healing
                                               Close Circle
_____

205

Appendix D: Suggested Reading

Energy Medicine, Donna Eden

You Can Heal Your Life, Louise Hay

Owning Your Own Shadow, Robert A Johnson

Handbook to Higher Consciousness, Ken Keyes, Jr

Ascension: Connecting with the Immortal Masters and Beings of Light, Susan G. Shumsky

Pleiadian Initiations of Light: A Guide to Energetically Awaken you to the Pleiadian Prophecies for Healing and Resurrection, Christine Day

The Twelve Rays of Light, Natalie Sian Glasson

Self Mastery Through the Twelve Rays: 12 Keys to Self Realization, Janet Houser

Hands of Light, Barbara Brennen

Awakening the Healer Within, Howard F Bati

Ascension Journey: A Handbook for Healing Through the Dimensions, Judith Marie McLean

Afterword

Activating Ascension is full of tools to assist you in living, healing and creating from your heart. It may take some time before you fully understand and are able to integrate its teachings. Be patient. Be aware of the subtle shifts and changes that will naturally arise after reading the book. Have faith, knowing that each small shift is moving you closer and closer to your intention. Focus on the step in front of you and allow your path to unfold.

For your first few Activating Ascension sessions, focus on one agenda at a time. Limit the number of obstacles to five and the number of techniques to three. This will help prevent you from feeling overwhelmed. Allow one session to fully process before beginning the next. Complete the follow-up every time. As you gain familiarity with the system, increase the number of agendas, obstacles and techniques to be all-inclusive.

Choose two or three of the techniques to complete as part of a daily routine to support the manifestation of your intentions. Intuitively choose a few that resonate the highest. Reevaluate periodically to ensure continued support.

If you would like additional help in learning the basics, consider having a private session with an Activating Ascension Practitioner or attending an Activating Ascension – D.I.Y. retreat. If you are being called to share this material with others, attend an Activating Ascension – Practitioner retreat. For more information about this, please visit www.activatingascension.com.

Author Bio

Dr. Kate Flynn lives in Knoxville, Tennessee with her husband, three children and two dogs. In her private practice, she offers her patients a comprehensive approach to care through Holistic Integration so that they may release the past with love and consciously create the reality they desire - free from pain, anxiety and depression. She sees patients in person and over the phone or internet. For more information about her work in private practice or to schedule a session, visit www.drkateflynn.com or email her at drkateflynn@gmail.com.

Dr. Kate also travels the country offering Activating Ascension retreats and publicly speaking about Activating Ascension and its ability to nurture conscious evolution and creation. More information about retreat dates and locations may be found at www.activatingascension.com. If you would like to host a retreat at your location, please submit your request via email.

Additional projects for Dr. Kate include the expansion of the Oracle Activation Card manuals into book form. She is also developing a system for the activation, restoration, reconfiguration and amplification of DNA. This will include a course, book and four additional sets of cards. Retreats for those desiring to become Activating Ascension practitioners, will be available in late 2014. Look for more information coming soon.

Made in the USA
San Bernardino, CA
20 March 2014